WOVEN STONE

Volume 21

SUN TRACKS

An American Indian Literary Series

Series Editors

Larry Evers and Ofelia Zepeda

Editorial Committee

Vine Deloria, Jr.

Joy Harjo

N. Scott Momaday

Emory Sekaquaptewa

Leslie Marmon Silko

WOVEN STONE

SIMON J. ORTIZ

THE UNIVERSITY OF ARIZONA

PRESS   TUCSON & LONDON

The University of Arizona Press
Copyright © 1992
Simon J. Ortiz
All Rights Reserved
♾ This book is printed on acid-free, archival-quality paper.
Manufactured in the United States of America.

97 96 95 94 93   6 5 4 3 2

Library of Congress Cataloging-in-Publication Data

Ortiz, Simon J., 1941–
    Woven stone / Simon J. Ortiz.
      p. cm. — (Sun tracks ; v. 21)
    ISBN 0-8165-1294-9 (alk. paper). — ISBN 0-8165-1330-9 (pbk. :
alk. paper)
    1. Acoma Indians—Poetry.   I. Title.   II. Series.
PS501.S85   vol. 21
[PS3565.R77]
810.8 s—DC20
[811'.54]   92-12507
                                             CIP

British Library Cataloguing-in-Publication Data
A catalogue record for this book is available from the British
   Library.

For my children,
Raho Nez, Rainy Dawn, and Sara Marie,
and their children—
and their children's children henceforth:

The stories and poems come forth,
and I am only a voice telling them.
They are the true source themselves.
The language of them is the vision
by which we see out and in and all around.

CONTENTS

A Good Journey   149

Fight Back: For the Sake of the People, For the Sake of the Land   285

WOVEN STONE

INTRODUCTION

Recently, I spoke to several groups of Laguna Pueblo Native American students at Laguna Elementary. After introductions and thanks for having me visit their school, I said in the Acoma Pueblo language, which is a linguistic sister to Laguna Pueblo, "Deetseyamah sthow-uh. Ehmi aistih dzuusteh, gaiyuh." Understanding that Deetseyamah was my home from where I had left that morning, a kindergarten boy raised his hand and said, "You speak Indian too?" "Hah uh," I said to the wide-eyed boy. "Yes. The Acoma language, which is almost the same as the Laguna language," I added. He smiled, and, looking at the children in a circle on the floor around me, I saw most of them smiling warmly.

I asked, "Do you know where Deetseyamah is?" None of them raised their hands or answered. Perhaps there were a couple who shyly wanted to, but they did not say anything. "Who knows where Mc-Cartys is?" I asked then, and many of the children quickly raised their hands. "Deetseyamah is where McCartys is. McCartys, Mericano dzehni shheyah ehmih ehgah. McCartys, that's its name in the American language," I told them. Realizing they knew or had learned where I was from, Deetseyamah, in their own language, they smiled again.

Standing before the children, I realized that what I do as a writer, teacher, and storyteller is to demystify language, and I smiled. Making language familiar and accessible to others, bringing it within their grasp and comprehension, is what a writer, teacher, and storyteller does or tries to do. I've been trying for over thirty years.

I didn't wonder that the boy, whose age I was almost fifty years ago, was so wide-eyed when I spoke to him in the Acoma language. Unfortunately, even with the advances made in bilingual education in the past twenty years, Native American languages are still not widely used in U.S. schools. I doubt if he even rarely heard his teachers and other school staff speaking in the Laguna language. That the children knew the name McCartys and where it was but did not know Deetseyamah, I understand. English language use is so commonplace now, and too often it has replaced native languages. McCartys is on New Mexico and Acoma and Laguna Pueblo maps, but not Deetseyamah or Kawaihkah, the native name for Laguna Pueblo. But when I told them the place name, Deetseyamah, and they understood it to be the same as McCartys, they realized they knew, *in their own language*, the place. It was not some strange, faraway village in a foreign country or another state but a community much like their own, and it was only several miles up the road. And they smiled in recognition of this as they grasped and understood this within the context of their family and community, heritage and culture, local history and landscape, and familiar language. I hope also the children realize that the name, Deetseyamah, and their language, whether it's mostly Laguna or mostly English, has as much validity, maybe more, as any other name and language.

As a writer who has used language, mostly English, in poetry, fiction, and essay for many years, I've tried to bring it within my grasp and comprehension and those of others, as I've said before—to demystify it essentially. I feel I've made English, the Mericano language, accessible to me, or at least some of it, but that was not always the case. To another group of Laguna Elementary students, I said, "When most of you started school, you likely spoke English and maybe Laguna as well. When I and others began school at McCartys Day School years ago, we did not speak, write, read, or understand English or very much of it." We did speak, understand, perceive, and feel in our native Acoma language, however, and if there is anything that has sustained me through my years of writing it is that fact, even though I do not speak the Acoma language as fluently and fully traditionally as others do in the Aacqumeh community.

Language and Consciousness

When I was born in the early 1940's, the first sounds of language I heard were those of the Aacqumeh hanoh—namely, my family and community. The Acoma people, according to oral traditional mythology, since leaving Kashkahtrutih, an immemorial time and place in the epic Acoma narrative of our development, have spoken our language. Even the language known and used in that ancient time and place is no longer spoken except in memory. "Kash," my mother told me, "means white. For example, kashshehshi. White corn. Now, there is another, more recent word, for it. 'Kash' is of the old language." Upon leaving Kashkahtrutih, it was required of the people to speak their own language which would come about from their intelligence, perception and expression, creativity, their consciousness.

Most of the first songs and chants I heard were in our native dzehni of Acoma, because that was what my mother and father and my grandparents mainly spoke—although I am sure I heard a small amount also of Mericano songs and childhood ditties from my older sisters who were in school. In our home and community of Deetseyamah as well as Acoma Pueblo as a whole, the main language was Acoma although, since Spanish colonization in the sixteenth century, some people spoke Spanish, as they did English when American occupation began in the 1840's. The cultural and linguistic integrity of Aacqu was relatively secure, though shaky, in the first half of the twentieth century, although it was constantly under attack by U.S. education, values, attitudes, influences, politics, and its economy—really by everything on all sides. Aacqu, like other Pueblos and Native American people, had to be constantly on the defensive, protecting its self-government, culture, livelihood, rights, land, language, its very lifeblood and spirit, everything. Within family and community, the Acoma language was a vital link to the continuance of the hanoh, the people, as a whole. The prayers, many of which are in song and chant, were for that, and I am sure the first murmur of prayer I heard and understood was in the Acoma language.

Years later, when I learned English well and began to use it fluently, at least technically and intellectually, I found myself "objectifying" my native language, that is, in translation. And it felt awkward, almost like I was doing something I was forbidden but doing it anyway. I've posed myself the frequent question: Is it possible to translate from the

Acoma language to another? Yes, I've insisted, but I'm not sure I am convinced of it or of how complete the translation is. Since we're all human with the same human feelings and responses to feelings, we understand and share hurt, love, anger, joy, sadness, elation, a gamut of emotions. However, human cultures are different from each other, and unique, and we have different and unique languages; it is not easy to translate from one language to another though we egotistically believe and *think* we can. And that is when I found myself objectifying my Acoma language and at emotional odds with myself.

When I was a very young boy, however, there was only one language and it was that commonplace, intimate speech carried on at home and community among family and others. And it was language that was specifically Acoma mostly, with a scattering of English words and phrases and even Spanish which had been "Acomized" and incorporated into the native tongue. Being very young, I had no need to distinguish language differences, nor was I aware of any until later; I simply understood and spoke "a language" with my parents, sisters and brothers, grandparents, aunts and uncles. This early language from birth to six years of age in the Acoma family and community was the basis and source of all I would do later in poetry, short fiction, essay, and other works, as a storyteller and as a teacher of creative writing and Native American literature.

Within our clan, the Eagle—Dyaamih hanoh—our family was close and supportive of each other, which was common throughout the Pueblo. A tightly knit clan and communal outlook and responsibility were encouraged, and these fostered close family and kin relationships. Unfortunately, this connectedness doesn't exist as strongly and integrally now as it did then, it seems. This closeness of family recalls for me a story I heard my oldest sister tell about a boy who could not talk.

The boy was four years old, well past the age when, normally, children talk or begin to. Other children his age were talking but the boy did not, and his older sisters were concerned. Why didn't he speak? Was he okay? They tried to get him to talk, saying Acoma words and urging him to repeat them, but he was silent. They had a grandfather who was a religious leader and healer; he knew the art and science of putting a person back into balance within the life of the Aacqumeh hanoh. So the sisters of the boy went to him, asking him to come and help their beloved brother to talk. "Maybe the boy has nothing to say," the grandfather told the girls. "Please, Grandpa," they pleaded. "Come and take a look at him; maybe you can help him." So the grandfather went to see the boy.

He called his grandson to come and stand before him, and he spoke to him. "Amoo uh, Nana, because of love for you, your sisters are worried about you not talking, and because of love for you, I have come to you. Perhaps, Nana, it is not time for you yet to speak, but you will when it is time. It is with language you will come about for yourself as a person and as a son of your family. It is with knowledge and words that you will know and express love for yourself and your people. Dzehni neeyah—with language—and with responsiblity for yourself and others, you will speak. That is how you will come about as a person. Amoo uh, Nana, nehmahshrou shruuh." Assuring the boy he would come to talk, the grandfather asked him to open his mouth widely, and, reaching into his levis pocket, he drew out a big, brass door key. He inserted the key into the boy's mouth and said, "Now, Grandson, you will speak." My sister concluded the story by saying, "Ever since then, we haven't been able to keep his mouth shut." And as I recall, she looked at me and smiled as if I had been that boy in the story.

It is that closeness, that intimacy enhanced by language, that I remember vividly, that was very apparent in our community of Aacqu, which is why I am pointing out and stressing language. The oral tradition of Native American people is based upon spoken language, but it is more than that too. Oral tradition is inclusive; it is the actions, behavior, relationships, practices throughout the whole social, economic, and spiritual life process of people. In this respect, the oral tradition is the consciousness of the people. I think at times "oral tradition" is defined too strictly in terms of verbal-vocal manifestations in stories, songs, meditations, ceremonies, ritual, philosophies, and clan and tribal histories passed from older generations to the next. When I consider the "idea" of Acoma oral tradition, I think of the interaction of the grandfather with his grandson, as well as what he spoke and what the story verbalizes as it is told. Oral tradition evokes and expresses a belief system, and it is specific activity that confirms and conveys that belief.

My book of poetry, *Going for the Rain*, written many years after my boyhood, expresses that closeness to a specific Native American way of life and its philosophy, and it is structured in the narrative form of an actual journey on the heeyaanih, the road of life, and its experience.

At the time of its writing, I felt this best expressed what I wanted to say with a literary perspective about Native American traditions, life, and experience. That boyhood closeness to life made me want to know it completely, to yearn for it, and to experience it deeply, and, paradoxically, it made me fear it as well and to avoid experiencing it—to run and hide from it in instances. Although not aware of it at the time of my youth, this was a prelude to the alcoholism I was to suffer later.

Starting school at the U.S. government McCartys Day School was looked forward to with both excitement and trepidation. Native American people have been faced with American schools since the 1870's or so as a federal policy. Though there were a few schools located in Native American communities or "Indian country" and American white teachers were sent out to educate Native American people, many, many children were sent away to federal and Christian mission boarding schools far from their homelands. The policy was to break or sever ties to culture, family, and tribe, to change indigenous people into "Americans." It was a severe and traumatic form of brainwashing, literally to destroy the heritage and identity of native people, ostensibly to assimilate them into an American way of life. "Mericano nehyahwihtraa skquwaahdrumaah," as the Aacqumeh hanoh would say. "To make us into American white people," as the Acoma people saw it. It was fearful to be faced by this, and my mother used to say that some grandparents would hide the children whenever a Mericano was seen driving a buckboard wagon toward Acoma. "They would sweep kahnee branches behind them to wipe away their tracks as they hid on the mesas," she said.

This official U.S. educational policy in its most extreme practice was implemented into the 1950's. My mother and father were sent before the 1920's to St. Catherine's Indian School and my older sisters, when I started school at McCartys, were at Albuquerque Indian School. It was exciting, however, "to go to school," even though I hardly spoke or knew any English except what I'd been coached to say by my sisters. I could say my "ABCs" and "Good morning, Miss Oleman," and I soon learned, "May I please be excused to go to the boys' bathroom," which is not easy for an Acoma child to say simply to go to the toilet. Most of us six- and seven-year-old children looked forward in any case to meeting and knowing each other, playing games, coloring pictures, and sharing a further sense of community and bonding which sometimes took the form of resistance against school and teachers. Though it was forbidden and punishable with a hard crack by the teacher's ruler across the back or knuckles, we continued to speak in our Aacqumeh dzehni, surreptitiously in the classroom and openly on the playground unless teachers were around. I have some fond memories of being in Peekqikqih, the beginning grade, although the reality of it then was harsher than my recollections.

Reading was fun. I quickly learned how to read. I know it was because I loved language and stories. All my life up to that point I loved the sounds of language and what was being told, and I would listen avidly to just about anything and I eavesdropped a lot, about which my father teased me by calling me a "reporter." As early on I associated reading with oral stories, it was not difficult to learn to read and subsequently to write. All in English, of course, as there was no such thing as bilingual education then, though now very minimally a few schools provide it. My mother read to us, too, perhaps even to a small extent before I started school, but my real interest and love of reading had to do with stories. I'd heard stories all my life, ranging from the very traditional to the history of Acoma-Mericano relations to current gossip. Stories were told about people of the Aacqumeh community, our relatives, both living and long ago, and there were stories of mythic people and beings who were wondrous and heroic and even magical. Some stories were funny, some sad; all were interesting and vitally important to me because, though I could not explain it then, they tied me into the communal body of my people and heritage. I could never hear enough of the stories. Consequently, when I learned to read and write, I believe I felt those stories continued somehow in the new language and use of the new language and they would never be lost, forgotten, and finally gone. They would always continue.

In writing *Going for the Rain* and later *A Good Journey*, I was very aware of trying to instill that sense of continuity essential to the poetry and stories in the books, essential to Native American life in fact, and making it as strongly apparent as possible. Without worrying about translation, I tried to relate them directly to their primary source in the oral tradition as I knew it. This quality of continuity or continuance I believe must be included and respected in every aspect of Native American life and outlook. I have often heard Native American elders repeat, "We must always remember," referring to grandmothers and grandfathers, heritage, and the past with a sense of something more than memory or remembering at stake. It is knowing present place and time, being present in the here and now essentially, just as past generations knew place and time whether they were Acoma, Lakota, or Mayan people. Continuance, in this sense, is life itself.

Since I was in school from Peekqikqih to the sixth grade at Deetse-yamah mostly, I was still within the hold of family and community; this was fortunate as many others had been taken away to school and still were at that time. I had a strong, continuing social-cultural connection with my people, for which I am grateful. "Education" and "learning" were stressed by parents, Acoma elders, and tribal leaders; they were deemed to be essential to our future and ability to live in the American way of life. Though it was not definitively pointed out, it was implied that education was necessary for employment and to live a bountiful, better life.

I began to feel stirrings of thoughts that focused upon our way of Acoma life compared with the American way of life. At moments, I even heard and perceived the idea that being Aacqumeh was not quite as good as being Mericano, although it was not until much later that I would find the words to describe and define racism, discrimination, and colonialism. However, the loving hold of its children by the Acoma family and community was insisted on, especially with reference to school. The social and cultural integrity and future of Aacqu would be maintained and strengthened by education and learning. Often and again, I heard elders repeat, "Go to school, stay in school, and get educated so you can help our people." Later when I learned the language to think and talk about colonialism, I knew the Aacqumeh hanoh were in resistance against the more destructive elements of American education and policy.

In 1954 when I was in the fifth grade, our family lived in Skull Valley, Arizona, for one year, and this was the first time I became surely aware of a world beyond Acoma. I knew there was one of course before then, since our teachers at McCartys were white and not Acoma people (Miss Oleman was from Missouri, wherever that was) and I read books (other than the school fare of Dick and Jane and Spot) where I learned of faraway places like South America, Africa, New York, Denver. And we had battery-powered radios that received broadcasts from El Paso and Shreveport which could have been on mysterious planets I read about. And definitely there were people howchaatya—"outside"—who were Mericano white, in great numbers and very different (we thought of them as rich and powerful), and there were Kashtu-urrlah (what we called our Hispanic neighbors), and Muurrlahtoh (African Americans), and Chinese (usually anyone who was Asian

American). There were also Lagunas and Navajos, Native American people nearby.

Acoma people had been outside, away from Aacqu, usually working, especially for the railroad and in the military, and they brought back knowledge and stories of California, Texas, Kansas, the Pacific Ocean, World War II, the Philippines, and Korea. My father had worked for the Santa Fe railroad since the late 1930's, and so I knew to some extent of places he had been, and it seemed to be a strange, very different, exciting, and somewhat scary world outside.

For me, this fear of the other world had to do not only with its difference from our familiar one but also with a feeling of not belonging in that world. It was a Mericano world where people were well off and in control, and we were Acoma people who were poor, who, I had been told, were taken care of by Shrahnaishtiyahshi Tsihchuu-hoochani, Our Father Big Government. As a fifth grader, a child of colonialism, I had doubts that Big Government would protect and take care of us if we left Aacqu. There were also other signs that it was not exactly safe away from Acoma. When young people, such as my older sisters (and later myself), were taken away by the busload every August for Indian boarding school, parents, grandparents, and other elders would advise and warn them of bad and dangerous influences they would face. These included alcohol use, bad people, and "wrong ways" in general. They were to remember family, home, community, and the ways of the Acoma culture. Many had been lost as a result of leaving home and of powerful influences, especially alcohol. Like many Native American communities and tribes, Acoma was afflicted by the destruction caused by liquor. Our family directly experienced the disease as my beloved father and other relatives abused alcohol, which caused family tension, arguments, distrust, fear, pain, all of the trauma of alcoholism.

Although I listened eagerly to stories about California or Arizona or other places, I also noticed there was something less than positive about them. I think it had to do with an awareness that it was socially difficult to live within the Mericano world and its way of life. I also noticed that Acoma people who went and lived howchaatya dhuuh—outside out there—were different, and when they came back home, they were different. They dressed, acted, talked differently, and even thought and felt differently, I sensed. I had perceived this in reading about American life in *Reader's Digest, True Romance,* "Our Weekly Reader," and school books with the famous Dick and Jane characters.

They lived with Mother and Father in a house with a lawn and white picket fence, and I knew they were different. But I really didn't know about Acoma people outside. Did they also come to live in houses with white picket fences and have dogs named Spot? So when we moved to Skull Valley where my father worked for the railroad, I had some knowledge of Mericano society, although a lot of it was wrought in my imagination and speculation. And we did not come to live in that mythical American home but in drab, substandard housing the railroad company provided for its section crew laborers.

Beyond and Not Beyond Acoma

Beyond Acoma, howchaatya dhuuh, was not the best of all possible worlds. For the first time in my life, away from our tiny enclave of Native and Mexican American railroad laborers' families, I felt like a minority. I couldn't talk about it, however, much less describe the feeling; up to then, I don't think I'd ever heard terms like "segregation" or "discrimination" or even "minority." But the feeling of being physically outnumbered was there, especially in that small farming and ranching community in north central Arizona and at the school where my younger sister and brothers and I were the only Native Americans. It was a tiny, one-room school, much smaller than the one at home, and I believe this helped us socially to "integrate" the all-white school, although we were regarded with curiosity and topical interest which was at times very uncomfortable. I was eleven years old, growing into adolescence, experiencing new sensations, finding girls enticingly interesting, and discovering new emotions especially about my identity. And I read voraciously just about anything I could get my hands on. The schoolteacher encouraged students to check books out of the three-shelf library, and I read *Robinson Crusoe, The Adventures of Huckleberry Finn*, and books by H. G. Wells and Arthur Conan Doyle, and many others.

Feeling like a minority in an American world was definitely not a good feeling. It meant feeling that you were looked at differently or feeling excluded, which did take place from time to time. There was something else, though, which didn't have much to do with race and culture. It had to do with being poor. My father as a railroad laborer was paid very low wages, and we got all our clothes and food from the company store, the Holmes Supply, on credit billed against my father's paycheck. We dressed as best we could but cheaply, and we kept our shoes until they were really worn.

As I was older then, likely inspired by magazines and books, I began to dream of the future, what I would do if I could and when I could. I took a job weeding and watering a garden for the local village store owner for whom my father worked on weekends, and I saved my pay of fifty cents a week. For a while I also sold mail-order hand salve for a company that offered prize merchandise after so many sales. From that enterprise, I got my first typewriter, an odd one-strike contraption that was more of a tin toy than anything. Perhaps that "typewriter" was part of a dream I may have begun to have, although I don't recall anything specific.

At that pre-adolescent age, experiencing new feelings from one moment to the next and being naturally inquisitive, I began to wonder about life. Questioning led to expressing, it seemed; for me, they were related. I feel lonely. Why am I lonely? What is loneliness? This is the way it feels. I feel love. Why? What is love? This is the way it feels to feel love. And then I think I began to write poetry, inspired by a mix of feelings and country-western and folk songs, strangely not Aacqumeh songs which I had grown up with. They were songs I heard on the radio, especially by Jimmy Rodgers and Hank Williams, or sung by my father who had a good voice. I liked songs that told stories, ballads, whether happy or tragic, and I began to write song lyrics and try out a fledgling, quavering voice in secret. And it was at that age, my yet-unseen future as a poet was launched with the publication of a Mothers' Day poem in the Skull Valley School newspaper.

We fared well as a family howchaatya dhuuh, although there were difficult and timorous times on occasion. I made close friends with my first non-Native American acquaintance, Boise, an itinerant Irish cowboy's son. We were the only fifth graders that year, and we shared a closeness as we went fishing, adventured, played cowboys and Indians (he, or his sister, was sometimes the Indian), and talked about girls. That year I learned the world outside was very big while Deetseyamah and our Acoma community were very small. I also learned gladly that, while not easy to do so, it was possible to live in the Mericano world and with some of its ways. White people were very different from us; sometimes they did strange and perplexing things, but generally if you watched and listened and considered them very carefully, you could understand them. As a people, I distrusted them less, although I was still wary of something that drove them willfully, aggressively, powerfully, and arrogantly. In that first time of living outside of Acoma, I didn't know it was that same drive that had settled its domain and rule over Native American lands and enforced an educational policy disguised as civilization.

After a last school year at McCartys, during which time I wrote juvenile poetry and songs, fantasizing being on stage or radio probably, I was sent to St. Catherine's Indian School in Santa Fe. I began to keep a diary, although it was more or less an accepted notion that boys didn't keep diaries. I did anyway, and since then I've kept a journal from time to time. In my diary, I wrote the usual notes about what I was doing and what was important: I got a letter from Mama today . . . I almost got in a fight with R. because . . . Said Hi to Dolores . . . Plaid socks are stupid . . . some of my feelings—though I think not much because, being shy and quiet mostly, I didn't talk or tell anyone about them hardly. Typically, I was the silent, stoic child of a dysfunctional family, community, and nation.

Now, many years later, I'm happy I was perceptive enough to keep a diary, write songs and poetry, read as much as I could (nuns encouraged it though I was supposed to only read books for lower grades—which I didn't limit myself to), and listen to stories. And remember stories, especially traditional Acoma oopehtahnee and tseekeenomah, old time stories, which I recall acting out in solitary sojourns in the hills and arroyos near St. Catherine's School. I smile now seeing that thirteen-year-old boy in a sandy arroyo long ago, loudly playing out the mythic story of the fierce, epic battle at Kashkahtrutih. My diary-keeping came to an end when one of the nuns caught me writing in it during study hall instead of doing my seventh grade science homework, and she took it. She didn't forbid me to keep a diary; she returned it and encouraged me. But I was self-conscious about it after that, and I quit for several years, although I kept writing poems. And by then, impressed with fiction I was reading by Hemingway, Saroyan, and Faulkner, and even plays by Shakespeare (although these were for upper grades at St. Kate's), I thought of writing stories.

I began writing brief, cursory passages, mainly scenes, descriptions, parts of plot, character sketches, and such. I didn't know anything about writing stories of course, except that stories were about people, what they looked like, what they did and how they acted, and maybe what they felt. At the time I don't think I made any solid, conscious connection between my piecemeal stories and those I read in books and magazines. I may have believed those stories came out of thin air and somehow got into print. And I know I didn't conceive anything about being a writer then because Acoma people were so distant from being Mericano that it was not even possible to consider such a thing— or dream of such. And yet I must have dreamed, or a dream was taking place which pulled me into it.

When I was working on the manuscript that was to become *Going for the Rain* and *A Good Journey* (I divided the book after I was told 300-page first major poetry collections weren't a good idea), I was very aware of my formative, adolescent years. In retrospect I discovered I had grown up educated or knowledgeable, though not literary in the strict sense, in the oral tradition, although I didn't know I was. In fact, I was just then discovering literature, and I was making, in my early teenage years, the initial connection, also a discovery, between litera- ture and my writing poetry and beginning stories. By then I was at Albuquerque Indian School because it was closer to home, Deetseya- mah, and my family. I had learned that AIS trained students in trades such as carpentry, sheet-metal work, agriculture, and, I think, mainte- nance. At that time of the early to mid 1950's, Native Americans were hardly encouraged to go into the professions but mostly into manual and technical trades, and so I wanted to learn a trade, really to become employable. That was the basic motivation; Native American young people were to grow up and go to work: get a job. It was the 1950's alright; there was even an early rock-and-roll song of that era with the lyric, "get a job." It was also the era of "Indian Termination" and "Relocation."

These were U.S. federal government programs applied as policies which darkly symbolize the oppression of Native Americans in the 1950's. Acoma Pueblo and other Native American people in the South- west were not directly affected by Termination as it was mainly ap- plied in Wisconsin and Oregon, but it was an effective threat that simply and bluntly said: The U.S. government will terminate all fed- eral services, ties, and recognition of Indian reservations and Indians will no longer be known as Indians. Relocation was simple too: the Bureau of Indian Affairs offered one-way tickets to jobs or training in urban areas such as Dallas, Chicago, San Jose, Los Angeles, Cleveland. The intent of the program, officially called Adult Vocational Training, was to depopulate rural Native American homelands.

The result was even more powerlessness, further fracturing and weakening of communities, and the loss of more people. No one could avoid and not notice the feelings current then. There was a sense of despair that even elders' urgings for the upkeep of tradition and heritage could not dispel easily. I recall at Aacqu that fewer and fewer people were taking part in religious activities, and those few were mostly older people. New Mexico legalized the sale of alcohol to Native Americans early in this period, an action that avalanched tremendous destructive personal, social, health, and legal problems. It was a sad time, and I don't exaggerate.

In spite of this, mainly because I was young and within my teenage world, I had dreams—or perhaps I began to let myself dream. I'd grown up in a harshly real world of poverty, on dry land—though beautiful—hard to make a living on, alcoholism in the family, and generally being faced by an anti-Native American America. And yet, maybe because of it, I dreamed of overcoming that and being respected and looked up to, being successful and rich, traveling to distant places, having a big car—some of those dreams were teenage fantasies heavily influenced by an American lifestyle and pop culture. I was at the same time aware also of changes taking place. It was a fast world, it seemed to me: one year it was the 1940's and then the next year it was a decade in the mid-1950's; one winter Acoma people used horses and wagons and the next spring some drove trucks and cars; my sisters had left home mostly and had begun to have children. The sand and rock trail to the top of Aacqu was suddenly paved so that trucks and cars could be driven on it; two Acoma young men had killed a state policeman; electric power lines sprang up overnight, and we had electric light for the first time. With astonishment, amazement, and occasional bewilderment, I noticed these things, and I thought about them seriously as a young Native American saw an older world change under his feet.

My grandfather had died early in the decade, and it seemed with his passing that something surely strong and significant was gone. Though I hadn't come to know him so well I sensed this, because as a boy I would go with him to tend our garden and fields, gather wood with him, and I would herd his sheep. I listened to his songs and stories, his advice and counsel spoken in a firm, steady, patient voice to his children and grandchildren, and I watched him working and moving about with the aged graceful motion of a man who has lived a long purposeful life. I was in awe of my grandfather actually, as he was a healer and spiritual leader who was highly respected by our people and other Native Americans who came to him for treatment and advice. In memory I see him in the midst of this rapidly changing time, especially as he spoke of seeing "Aishtenhower" in Gallup eighty miles west of Acoma where Dwight Eisenhower made a quick presidential campaign stop, described by my grandfather as a large crowd of people looking at a Mericano who was going to be the Tsihchuu-hoochani. The world and times were changing, and I could feel myself changing with them. Watching and studying these changes, I began to think of the possibility that I had something to do with them, and I wondered about the relationships between people and circumstances.

I wanted to retain the memory of my grandfather and grandmother and the grandfathers and grandmothers before them and the times they had gone through. I had heard the oral history of the Spanish coming, the taking of land by them and later by the Mericano, the Treaty of Guadalupe de Hidalgo that was apocryphal to the native people, the coming of the railroad, the struggles to keep land and a way of life and sovereignty as a people. I became aware that I was living in a time and place that was the result of change in which Native American people had a role and that we had a role now. Though I didn't understand exactly how this role worked or could work, I felt it was there and nothing could change it. Therefore it was important to remember the past so that I could learn from it what there was to do in the present. Although Aacqu was the only real place I'd ever known, I had learned it was only a small tribe, one of many across the nation. At Indian School, I had met Native Americans from different communities who spoke different languages. A sense of heritage and identity was becoming apparent to me, and it was the beginning of a definite purpose in being Native American—Indian, as we commonly knew ourselves then. With this forming abstractly in my mind and tangibly aware of it in emotional reactions, I felt a pride and love for my race and culture, though paradoxically at the same time there was a bothersome self-consciousness about being Indian. By then I was out of Albuquerque Indian School and at Grants High, a public school with an integrated student body.

A Good Journey, a collection of narrative poetry, is an evocation literarily and intellectually of my explicit emotional awareness of that time. The book is based upon the oral tradition, specifically the oral voice of stories, song, history, and contemporary experience. Though I didn't write any of it during the time I speak of, a sensitivity about remembering, an awareness of heritage and culture, having a purposeful identity, coming to know I had some control of my fate were all part of forming a commitment to acknowledge and to be who I was as an Aacqumeh person. Although I would not articulate it until much later in my life, I felt my heritage and culture and how they were expressed were the basis of who I was and how I came into being as a human being. The poetry in this book is styled as a storytelling narrative ranging from a contemporary rendering of older traditional stories to current experience: from Grandmother Spider to my children, from Coyote to being in the Veterans Hospital for alcoholism treatment (which as a teenager I had no idea was going to happen).

A commitment as an Acoma Native American, however, was strong and firm, although at times, like others I'm sure, I was prey to self-doubt and I wavered. Self-questioning was a part of my self-expression in any case, as I've explained before. And by now, I was consciously writing, going back over it, revising, and even showing it to my girlfriend. My dreams and fantasies were less momentary now; at sixteen and seventeen years of age, I was imagining myself, romanticizing the image I'm sure, as a writer later on in life. I may even have been planning books and magazine articles. I was even more of a reader, heavily into recent and current poets and novelists like Carl Sandburg, Dylan Thomas, and Sinclair Lewis, Flannery O'Connor, Carson McCullers, Sherwood Anderson, Saul Bellow, Ernest Hemingway, William Faulkner, John Updike. I had read or was reading a lot of the American and European classics by Shakespeare, Dante, Flaubert, de Maupassant, Tolstoi, Blake, Eliot, James Joyce, and such. Although I was acquiring wide knowledge of this literature and non-Native American thought, I also knew I would never strive to be anything other than an Aacqumeh hahtrudzai, a Native American of my homeland and people. When I read and ingested the ideas, views, feelings, and visions from this literature, again I strongly felt the stories, songs, experiences, feelings, and visions of my own indigenous people were somehow continued in the aesthetic, intellectual, and emotional experience and knowledge I was gaining.

Stories, poems, histories did not come out of thin air—that's what I came to acknowledge and decide. They came from the thoughts, feelings, and experiences of my people, from their voices, and they came from thoughts, feelings, experiences, and writings of people different from us but who were human beings like us. Shakespeare, Blake, Homer, Nelson Algren, James Baldwin, Richard Wright were human voices and writers. People and experience; people and circumstance—I pondered these for hours, I'm sure with a mix of excitement, dismay, and too much seriousness. And I wrote my thoughts in my journal, which I had begun to keep again, and in poetry and stories.

As a high school student, I was active and busy with school, athletic, social, community activities and also with work as our family planted and kept a garden, but I always managed to have time to read and write. I was academic-minded; I liked to discuss ideas and be involved with intellectual endeavors. I felt especially an awareness that our Acoma people and culture were in a fateful period of our destiny, and because I had grown up with the indigenous dictum of "helping our people," I began to realize I had a part in that destiny. Though I can't say that my writing was motivated by that realization or came from it directly, there was a notion urging me to express myself.

Because I was pretty impressionable then, when I came across the writings of the Beat Generation, especially those of Allen Ginsberg and Gary Snyder, I was struck as if by a revelation. It was "experience" I noticed, the idea of experience, writing from and about experience, and writing as experience. Snyder's poetry particularly had aspects of Zen Buddhist philosophy I related to because they were similar in many ways to Native American spiritual knowledge and belief; reading the poetry and having in mind writing as experience, it was as if I'd known Buddhism all my life. And the revelation that was brought to light for me was that as an Acoma person I also had something important, unique, and special to say. I did not, however, express myself in writing immediately about it; then I recognized it and gladly shared a sense of comradeship and association with the philosophy, literature, and the poet. At age eighteen, I don't know how much of my writing was inspired by the Beats but I recall being overly impressed by Jack Kerouac's prose which I took to mean "it was alright to be alright." My writing was then focused on everyday items and topics such as stones, lizards, ants, rusty cans, birds, ordinary thoughts about them, stars that caught my attention, and ideas about fate and future. My beginning fiction, which I wrote more than poetry, was about struggling people, mostly poor, enduring, hardworking, caring, and they were not identified as to ethnicity and culture, certainly not Native American or Indian or Acoma.

Why not?—it may be asked. Isn't that a contradiction? No, it's not, I have to say and answer why. As a Native American I had grown up in a certain way culturally, socially, spiritually, and politically. I was an Aacqumeh person in a community that was tiny compared with the

larger world outside which was American society, the United States. In
a sense, as a colonized indigenous person, I was more familiar with the
larger society than my own because that society in influence, numbers,
and political economic impact was overwhelming. And very dominant,
especially in the latter 1950's even though the Civil Rights struggles
by African Americans and other minorities were active. Although I
identified myself as an Acoma Native American and was aware of mi-
nority issues, I have to admit my views and concepts in large part were
those of the dominant society. I loved my family, people, community,
yet I was also swayed by powerful influences of the outside and even
yearned and sought for those "Mericano ways." This is not an unusual
phenomenon, as anyone from a colonized people can say. This phe-
nomenon is why heritage, culture, even native languages, and identity
are ignored, forgotten, and lost. It is not by choice that it takes place; it
is literally by force that it happens. Native American people have expe-
rienced it since the so-called "discovery" of the New World as they've
run the gauntlet of genocide and enslavement, Manifest Destiny, U.S.
citizenship, and assimilation.

You can't help but be persuaded by attitudes, values, viewpoints to
a major extent, no matter how loyal you are to your heritage, no matter
if Native American elders remind you constantly that you belong to
your people. Just as it claimed land and sovereignty, American society
and culture can claim your soul. People in my early fiction had souls
as hardworking farmers and laborers, but they did not have faces,
thoughts, or language as Native Americans, although they were not
identified as white Americans either. There was an unconscious con-
tradiction, however—a result I would say of my youthful naiveté:
while I knew myself as an Acoma and was inspired by an emerging
ethnic cultural nationalism, I did not write about being Native Ameri-
can. This could be taken to mean a denial of my Native American
identity and heritage. In a sense it is, principally for the reasons above.
Among writings I have on hand, loose-leaf notes, pocket note pads,
tablets, typed papers, etc., I find hardly any ethnically identifiable
writing from that period. That would not come about until years later
when I was in my twenties and had developed a firmer political con-
sciousness. But I was somewhat aware of this unconscious denial; I felt
uncomfortable about it, especially in instances when I was being de-
fensive about my Native American identity and outlook.

I recall an occasion which is humorous now in retrospect that oc-
curred when I was almost nineteen and about to graduate from high

school. At Grants High, I was an accomplished student; such things as Boys State, class officer, co-captain of the football team, all-state in sports, Mr. Grants High, and Senior Honor Boy came to me. I was self-conscious about the recognition but I was also proud, as were my mother and father. The town of Grants and the school were mostly all white, and Native Americans were a definite minority along with Hispanics, so part of the pride had to do with my achievement as a Native American. When I was named Honor Boy at a banquet at school, my parents went with me, and we sat among other students and their parents.

We were all kind of nervous as we were the only Indian family there, and I noticed that my beloved mother was speaking only in English. She was bilingual in Acoma and English but she insisted on using only English that evening. At home she spoke mainly Acoma, but at the banquet she conversed with my father and me in English. I was surprised, shocked, and mystified; I wanted her to be natural, the Acoma woman she always was, and comfortable. And, frankly, I was upset, although I didn't say anything. Not till much later did I understand and appreciate what she was likely going through with her nervousness, anxiety, and memories of past experience howchaatya dhuuh in America. Fondly now, and smiling about my own over-eager awareness and defensiveness about my heritage, I recall that occasion with my beloved, proud parents.

Being conscious, and admittedly self-conscious at moments, of being Native American and having formed a sense of purpose about it and by then confirmed in the idea of writing as experience, I made the decision to be a writer. The thought of it as a career, profession, job, or whatever it could be called (I didn't know; I didn't even know what it involved) had been gestating for several years. I also said I would like to be an organic chemist, but I don't think I really wanted to be. Mainly, I wanted to read and read and read and think and discuss ideas and write. Though it's not clear that being Native American had definitely to do with the decision, I believe my pondering, questions, even my self-consciousness sparked the decision and pushed me toward it.

How to become and be a writer I didn't know; I hadn't ever read any writer's autobiography which could give me a clue. It didn't matter; I simply had arrived at the decision over a period of some time, and I knew that's what I wanted to do. But how? Besides reading and studying the writing of others, how did that work? I didn't know and sometimes I still don't know. College? Experience? Adventure? Falling in love? So I went to work in the uranium industry which for several

years had been extracting uranium ore from lands in the Southwest
and processing it at several millsites.

Being and Reality

Grants, in mid-northwestern New Mexico, and the region nearby
which includes Deetseyamah, Acoma Pueblo, several small Mexican-
American villages and towns, and Laguna Pueblo were beset by the
twentieth-century corporate industrial age, principally intensive open-
pit and underground mining—and ore-processing by the same giant
mining and energy corporations, including Kerr-McGee, Phillips Petro-
leum, Anaconda, and Homestake. Uranium mining had begun in the
1940's in the Four Corners area, and in 1952–53, Jackpile Mine, the
world's largest open pit uranium mine, opened on Laguna land. It em-
ployed Laguna laborers and semiskilled workers and was a boon to the
Pueblo for a while.

By 1960 when I began work for Kerr-McGee, underground mining
was at full throttle west and northwest of our homeland. Acoma men
and boys as well as others from the region went to work for the mining
and processing companies. We were a source of cheap labor because of
high unemployment. In decades before, there was a small-scale timber
industry, as well as some agricultural employment (mostly in picking
and packing carrots), railroad work, and tourism which continues to-
day, but nothing quite like this uranium boom. Aacqumeh hanoh as
a whole felt better off financially because of mining wages earned,
though I noticed there was less attention given to gardens, fields, or-
chards, and livestock. Having grown up poor, I know I felt personally
better off, was able to help my family, and I bought a car shortly.

Working with men who came from West Virginia, Colorado, Mon-
tana, and other mining regions and men from the oil fields of Okla-
homa, Texas, and the Gulf of Mexico was quite an experience for me
as I was eager to learn about different people. These men were mostly
working-class whites, definitely not intellectuals for the most part,
who were hardworking, earnest, loyal to their group, even clannish,
opinionated and blunt in their speech. They also, I noticed, were not
far removed from land-based backgrounds, and I identified with them.
In fact, I later modeled some characters in my writing after workers I
knew. And definitely *Fight Back: For the Sake of the People, For the
Sake of the Land* was set within the context of the uranium industry
in the early 1960's. Its stories and poems, although not written until
twenty years later, as the industry was winding down, were being

formed in my experience and perception of it in my early adulthood. It was a time when I was aware of being on my own, forming my views, confirming my feelings, and becoming aware politically. I was unsure of myself, of course, and often, with the men I rode carpool and worked with, I found I was shy and awkward. When I was asked a question, especially related to Native American ways and views, I said, "I don't know." I may have known what to answer but sometimes I didn't answer. Saying "I don't know" was a way of hiding, I suppose, and responding defensively. For the first time I was also on my own as an Acoma young person in a culturally and racially mixed society.

Politically, Acoma Pueblo was feeling its way in the dark. It seemed to feel the community was inadequately fit to compete with others, particularly the outside, notably state government agencies and representatives, business, and a federal government that was supposedly our guardian. That is why there was the continual urging by tribal leaders and elders to get educated so we'd be more qualified and have some power and control. I felt this hunger for a semblance of control, especially with regard to land, water, tribal government, and tribal income, and, because there was little evidence of control, it almost seemed like none. Because I was loyal and defensive about my Acoma and Native American heritage, youthfully I asserted a personal sense of control of my destiny, mainly through independent behavior, opinions, and reflections on changes in Native American life, more seriousness about literature and writing, and trying to learn about the American political process. This assertion was clearly from a Native American standpoint, though not yet as a Red Power stance. It was my effort, especially in light of national social changes gaining momentum, to try to understand if American politics were beneficial to Native Americans and other minorities.

Although I felt a pull toward the Civil Rights movement and the Kennedy charisma, I was independent in viewpoint. Mainly, I was concerned about social changes affecting Native American people, changes we were making in the dark because of the lack of education and control due to a lack of a significant part in sociopolitical dynamics. Like some Aacqumeh elders, I felt we had little say-so in the changing social and political swirl around us, and if we didn't speak up and act, we would become dizzy, confused, and swallowed up. Economically, it was the same; though we seemed to be better off, we were also becoming more dependent upon wages, commercial items from the outside, and purchasable satisfaction and comfort. In all, we seemed to be less certain, solid, and whole as Native Americans. This definitely related to political issues and process which we had to take part in if we were to have control of our destiny.

As a young working man, independent-minded, becoming more aware explicitly and overtly of racial and ethnic discrimination, seeing that Black people as minorities were doing something about their part in social change, and being sensitive, I was angry. Like other colonized indigenous youth, I had been quietly seething for many years. Being obedient usually to authority and respectful of elders, I kept my feelings to myself. Now I found myself more open with views and emotions, though also guarded. (Also I still said from time to time, "I don't know.") I recall the anger at my parents and grandparents, blaming them for not warning us and not protecting us from American life and its people, and I was upset at Acoma leadership for not fighting harder to hold our land and water (That's why, I thought and said, we have so little now!)—and it was all due to not being involved. I was youthfully foolhardy, naive, and impulsive. I wanted us to fight back with a strong sense of our culture, language, and identity, and it seemed to me that we weren't doing so—at least not in my estimation. My concern turned inward and became too thoughtful, alienated, egotistical, and careless. Though I worked with others and was distantly involved with community activities, I was less social. My writing, which I was serious about by then, became a way of being private. And, ironically, though I spoke of speaking out and being involved, I did suppress feelings too, stuffing them, and becoming aloof. I also began to drink heavily for the first time.

Alcoholism I had known all my life. As a child I was traumatically afraid of the behavior of my father and others under the influence of alcohol. I just didn't understand it, yet I knew its fearsome, destructive impact first hand. Essentially, I denied it, which is a way of protecting against it—pretending it wasn't there—causing it to have an unnecessary mystique and a real power psychologically. This power and mystique, strangely, to alcoholics and potential alcoholics becomes a magnet; its very appeal seems to be its fearful nature, which says something about alcoholism being a disease of insanity. I know that I used drinking to exert the independence I wanted; I seemed to feel more capable of individual, decisive action. It made me comfortable where ordinarily I would be uneasy and nervous. Also, as a brash, beginning writer with a feverish artistic burning inside, I was egocentric—I could do anything I wanted, no one could tell me of the dangers of alcohol use, and I was arrogant enough to think I could control it. Besides, great writers like Dylan Thomas, Hemingway, Thomas Wolfe, Malcom Lowry drank a lot—so I could too. In my early twenties, I wasn't about to think that alcohol might have done them in. I believed in their greatness and in drinking as a part of that. Romanticizing that image of the guzzling, garrulous writer, I experienced my initial early troubles with drinking, insisting that I just needed to be more careful. That should have pointed out to me strongly the power that it had over me, and from that point on alcohol would know me very well.

The early half of the 1960's for me was a vigorous mixture of self-discovery as a young writer, finding myself interested and concerned about social changes, being a college student for a while, and serving in the U.S. Army. I kept a haphazard journal, wrote quite a lot of rambling, long passages that might have been never-ending stories, and some poetry. In my second college year, I definitely knew I was not chemist material, instead choosing to think of myself as an "intellectual"—mainly I wanted to read, think, and write. This period of time set for me a goal and commitment, though still forming at the same time, to be a writer—at last I felt it was possible to put a dream into reality.

The 1960's had begun as a Camelot era: dreaming was allowed, the Civil Rights struggle was freeing everyone, and I was no exception as a dreamer. Dr. Martin Luther King, Jr. and Muhammad Ali were spokesmen for the dream of that age. It was okay to be justly angry, and oppressed people had the right to demand social, economic, and political changes and go out on the road and streets to vent their suppressed rage. But the dark oppposite of the dream was there too, biding its stealthy task, and its deadly bullets struck down one of the generation's first heroes, President John F. Kennedy, and slipped back into hiding until the next time. The dream though shaken was not ended as the poor and working class, especially minorities, did not let it die, and the Third World national liberation struggles had come awake. These were inspiration and food for my hungry mind; thoughts and ideas about them filled my notebooks and my "Dear America" letters which occur to me now as the first work I thought of as a book manuscript. The letters were intensely emotional diatribes about the madness

called America and were written in the era of the Cuban invasion fi-
asco, the brutal authoritarian put-down of Black demonstrations in the
South, and the Kennedy assassination.

I took Army basic training in Louisiana, and I recall my first racial
experience in the South one weekend when a Mexican American
buddy and I went to Lake Charles. We had both grown up in the South-
west, where we knew discrimination existed, and we knew of social
conditions in the South. But somehow we thought because we were
not from the South and not Black, though we were dark-skinned, we
were immune from racism. We were mutually ignorant. We were
hitchhiking out of Leesville when a Black sergeant stopped his car to
pick us up. He glared at us for a moment before driving on, and then he
growled, "It's not good for you guys to be out on a road like this." He
paused, and I was nervous. And then shaking his head slowly, he said,
"Dark people get killed around here." My buddy and I were very quiet,
sheepishly looking at each other out of the corners of our eyes. Return-
ing from Lake Charles, we went to the bus station to take the bus
back. There we saw the "Whites Only" and "Colored Only" signs on
the restrooms. I thought that time was over, but I was wrong; it was
still the right time and way in Lake Charles. When I needed to take a
leak, I went into the Colored Only side feeling like that boy years be-
fore howchaatya dhuu in Skull Valley. This was what my letters, "Dear
America," were about.

Facing reality has never been easy for me; it's always been more of a
confrontation, and too often I have turned away. Being Native Ameri-
can is a major factor in this, as perhaps it's been for others. Even know-
ing ourselves as Native Americans is a question and an issue. In my
early years, my people knew themselves as Aacqumeh and we were
Intyuuh—Indian. In the past ten years of the 1980's, the term Native
American has become current, and I'm using it predominantly in this
introduction. What happened to Indians? As colonized indigenous
people our terminology too often is not our own. Columbus over eagerly
thought he was in Asia, so the story goes, and he called us "Indios."
The reality is that we are who we are in our own consciousness and
the language that we express it in. Aacqumeh stuudhah and my people
Aacqumeh tsaa-ah.

In an America, particularly the United States, which is overwhelm-
ingly present every day, in every social, political, cultural, economic,
psychological way, it's hard not to feel as if you're *confronting* a reality
that's so powerful you can't expect it to recognize you. Especially if

you are a people who has been historically subjected to the meanest, cruelest treatment by social and economic forces backed up by military power, with the result being a feeling of no self-esteem, insignificance, powerlessness, and of being at the mercy of powers beyond your control. So what is the solution, the way out of this and the way to becoming whole, healthy, and positive? I believe a major part of the way has to do with the consciousness we have of our selves, the language we use (not necessarily only native languages but the consciousness of our true selves at the core of whatever language we use, including English), and our responsible care for and relationships we have with our communities and communal lands. This is the way as Native Americans we will come into being as who we are within the reality of what we face.

Perhaps, in some ways, I am still like that young man years ago who was foolishly angry because he felt his tribal leaders and elders had not fought hard enough to save land, self-government, and people. However, I insist that our present-day conscious and purposeful involvement in social change must continually be there, as I believe it has been before. This goes all the way back to anti-colonialist resistance by native people of the Northeast, the Indian Pueblo revolt against the Spanish, Tecumseh's struggle to unite people from the Great Lakes to the Gulf of Mexico, and Crazy Horse's and Sitting Bull's heroic efforts to lead their people in saving the Great Sioux Nation. It's been there in the more recent Fishing Rights, Land Claims, Treaty Rights struggles which have overlapped from one generation to the next, from one era to the following one, including the 1960's to the present. This consciousness and involvement will be there if the language of it is expressed openly and insightfully. This is true in regard to Native American–U.S. relations and history and capitalism's money-power hunger. We need to insist on Native American self-sufficiency, our heritage of cultural resistance, and advocacy for a role in international Third World de-colonizing struggles, including recognizing and unifying with our indigenous sisters and brothers in the Americas of the Western Hemisphere.

A major source of this language of coming into being comes from the work of writers such as myself. Since the late 1960's, Native American writers and thinkers have addressed such serious concerns and ideas to some extent, advocating ethnic cultural expression, describing Native American ways and thought, analyzing and criticizing Western civilization, and promoting indigenous heritage and language.

But unfortunately we are also easily distracted and diverted. We have not yet thoroughly and honestly focused on critical issues that are related directly to our identity and existence as human beings who are Native Americans, citizens of the United States, carriers of a unique cultural heritage, and who are faced with ethnocentrism among ourselves and racism. Since coming into and forming consciousness is the source of coming into existence as who we are and maintaining it, it is critical to deal with these issues.

My last marriage was to Marlene, an Anglo-American, who is the mother of Sara, our daughter. We dearly love her and, though divorced, we are trying to raise her to know and respect her ethnic, racial, and cultural heritages. Sara is not unusual among Native Americans; we are a mixed people. In fact, my son is mixed tribally and my other daughter is tribally and racially mixed. Recently (much later after the years I've been telling about in becoming a writer), Marlene pointed out to me that I've never included her as a person in my writing, that in fact I'd excluded her on purpose. She added, "And I know why, too—racism." Spontaneously, my reaction was that it wasn't true, that not mentioning her had nothing to do with racism. And I was upset she was implying I was racist. As defensive people, too often reactive, culturally conscious of their identity, loyal to their immediate community, tightly knit as an ethnic group, Native Americans are sometimes described as racist in outlook. We are not, but we wonder: too often we question the validity of our ethnic cultural stance and our heritage, and I think we should look at racism itself.

Racism has to do with social and political power, as I understand it, achieving, maintaining, and using it exploitatively, manipulatively, and aggressively. The power is used and intended to strongly secure and tightly hold the position of the user, and it is used along with a philosophical belief. Europe for example, namely through England and Spain, two main proponents of the power of domination, when it expanded its hegemony to Africa and America, started with a belief in its advanced status (they were civilized) and God (they were direct descendants of the Christian God, having been made in his image). This belief system was expressed in the arts, government, economy, schools of thought, morals and religion, family and male-female roles, the social-cultural system in general; it was natural for the British and Spanish to assume they were superior and to expect others, especially the natives of lands they claimed, to recognize their superiority. And when they did not, they rationalized they could do whatever it took to make the natives submit to superior reason, decision, and authority; eventually, they would believe in European superiority and power, it was reasoned.

Native American people were mystified and perhaps somewhat enchanted by this belief system of insistent superiority. Early colonizers of the Northeast had a difficult and hungry time in the wilderness; they needed help, and from chronicles of the time it's known that indigenous people helped them. Without aid and even dependence upon native help and knowledge, the Spanish in the South would likely have perished also. In spite of this obvious helplessness and ineptitude, Native Americans noticed the persistence, fortitude, and dogmatism of the Europeans; they were powered by a willing belief in their superiority and God. Though stated here somewhat simplistically, it came down to this: the English and Spanish would face all odds and circumstances with this belief.

Aside from being mystified, Native Americans initially accorded respect to the Europeans' belief in their God. And they acknowledged the differences in how the foreigners dressed, spoke, and behaved. There were many different Native American tribal peoples who dressed differently, had different languages, and acted in certain ways particular to their culture—so Europeans initially were treated likewise. Native Americans had a religious belief that depended upon a spiritual and material relationship with creation and the earth. People got what they needed to live from the land-earth, and they gave back, with their work, responsibility, and careful use of natural resources, what the land needed. Their creators gave them life, and they, with prayer, meditation, and ritual, gave back life; they received and gave. This belief was a system of reciprocity in every respect, and the relationship they had with creators and earth was the guiding rule which was applied to their social communal system. And they assumed Europeans would also abide willingly and sensibly by this system, which would insure everyone's continuity and existence. Sadly, this was not to be. The European urge for domination, compounded by capitalism's quest for profit, overwhelmed and submerged everything and everyone not only with language, philosophy, behavior, economy, government but with violence and brute force when rhetorical persuasion failed. Soon Native Americans feared Europeans and gave way to European conquest; since then, they have known racism as a system used to control them and other ethnic racial minorities in the United States.

Ethnocentrism, or tribalism, among Native Americans is an outcome of racism and colonialism. As victims of colonialism who have been made to feel powerless, Native Americans strive desperately to gain some control of their lives and destiny, to gain a positive feeling of self. It is a simple, basic belief in one's culture, language, image, community, heritage that provides this feeling. In effect, it comes from fighting racism which has taken away the positive feeling; it is an effort to reverse racism's result by regaining belief in self. Unfortunately, the fight against racism and the outcome result too often in a narrow focus that is defensive, egocentric, and exclusive of other people. It creates disunity, fragmented purpose, rivalries and jealousies, blinds Native Americans to each other and other Indigenous People in the hemisphere, and it makes us ultimately invisible because it makes us doubt our identity as a united Indigenous People.

Fiercely fighting for so long against becoming invisible, we have to fully learn about our victimization by racism and ethnocentricism so we don't make ourselves invisible. In my own insistence on being visible as a Native American, I have too often excluded inadvertently other people and cultures from my writing because of ethnocentricity, the outcome of racism. Marlene was indirectly right in her comment about it, saying, "And I know why, too—racism." I am grateful to her for bringing about the opportunity for me to think about it, because it is a significant and crucial topic we Native Americans need to look at.

Fighting On and Fighting Back

There are many issues and concerns that Native American writers need to focus upon, and they must take the opportunity to do so when they appropriately can. In this present exposition, constraints of time and space have limited my discussion to my early writing career, some ideas on language, present concerns of Native American writing, and relating the discussion to the three books in *Woven Stone*. It has been only since the 1960's that Native American writers have been published to any extent; before then it was as if we were truly invisible, truly the "vanishing Indian" of the U.S.A.'s vainglorious wish. I still insist we must be involved critically; art and politics do mix, though it may be a volatile mixture and conservatives may be uneasy about it. In 1980, I published *Fight Back: For the Sake of the People, For the Sake of the Land*, which I've updated for this volume. It is a literary work intended to be a political statement about what was happening to our land and lives in the Acoma-Grants-Laguna region where the uranium industry was most active. I had looked back three hundred years at the Pueblo Revolt of 1680 when the dispossessed, oppressed poor led by the Pueblo Indian people rose against the civil, religious, and military rule of the Spanish. The rebellion was against theft of land and resources, slave labor, religious persecution, and unjust tribute demands. The people and land had been colonized and dominated for almost a hundred years by Spanish power, and there seemed to be no other recourse but to overthrow oppressive Spanish rule. And the people, who included most of the native Pueblos, detribalized Indians, Mulattoes and Mestizos, and Apaches and Navajos, were successful. From 1680 to 1692, our homeland was free of the dire social conditions that had caused the people to revolt.

Three hundred years later, some of those same conditions existed, a result this time of a modern-day American society and the uranium industry. Corporate mining companies required cheap labor—we were it. Grants, the mostly white boomtown, and its businesses wanted profits—they took our hard-earned low wages. "Bad influences" sold us liquor and turned us against our values. American public schools hardly mentioned us except as tribal participants, in fact hindrances, in American progress and development. Christianity still mainly missionized, its members praying for our still-heathen souls. The American political-economic system was mainly interested in control and exploitation, and it didn't matter how it was achieved—just like the Spanish crown had been ignorant of people's concerns and welfare. I understood the reason for the Pueblo Revolt of 1680, and with poetry and prose I tried to express my perception and hope for the present and future in *Fight Back*.

Fighting back is fighting on, and this is the continuance I referred to earlier. It must be a part of every aspect of Native American life and outlook. As a boy coming to read and write in English, I felt a continuing coming into being as an Acoma person because I knew my consciousness continued in the new language and it would never be lost and finally gone. Native American intellectual and literary voices are essential to the Americas. I use the phrase "coming into being" to also mean coming into being as an Indigenous People of the Americas, and truly this is coming into reality within the reality we now face. We cannot turn away, for if we do we disappear; we would no longer exist. Indigenous thought and writing are essential now in the 1990's and into the next century. Especially is this true in terms of a unified vision by all the Indigenous People of this hemisphere; we must realize this and recognize each other personally, socially, communally, and politically. Canadian and Ecuadoran poets, Brazilian and Mexican novelists, U.S. and Peruvian playwrights, all indigenous writers as intellectuals, leaders, and spokesmen and women for their people, culture, and native consciousness are vital for this vision to emerge.

Facing and living in reality is living in the here and now. Being present with and for ourselves, being responsible to ourselves and, consequently, for our role in social struggles and changes in the Americas is a major part of this. Too often we have, as victims of colonialism, longed for the past nostalgically and whimsically, although there is appropriate importance in what elders say about remembering the past. And too often we look abstractly at a romanticized future that is impractical. As Native American people, sisters and brothers to all Indigenous People of the Americas, we must not forsake the present reality of our continuing lives, families, communities, cultures, languages, consciousness, self-governing nations, and political-economic struggles for our lands and reciprocal self-sufficiency. Loss of land and people and self-respect has been a heavy burden on our spirits; too often this is an excuse for low self-esteem and self-blame, causing us to be like that boy years ago who didn't talk, even causing us to fear facing reality and to run and hide.

When this fear overwhelms us, making us run and hide, this is when we are most susceptible to self-destruction, especially by the disease of alcoholism from which I have suffered personally and from which I am newly recovering. As an Aacqumeh hahtrudzai and a writer, I believe that being real in a real world is loving and respecting myself. This I believe has always been the true and real vision of Indigenous People of the Americas: to love, respect, and be responsible to ourselves and others, and to behold with passion and awe the wonders and bounty and beauty of creation and the world around us.

Native American writers must have an individual and communally unified commitment to their art and its relationship to their indigenous culture and people, especially with regard to social, cultural, political-economic health and to progressive development. I believe, with this commitment, we have insight and compassion in common with Pablo Neruda, Meridel LeSeur, Ernesto Cardenal, Richard Wright, Nazim Hikmet, who have written with honest and basic love of land and people and their struggles. In this, there is something more than survival and saving ourselves: it is continuance. The United States will not be able to survive unless it comes to truly know and accept its indigenous reality, and this is its continuance. Through our poetry, prose, and other written works that evoke love, respect, and responsibility, Native Americans may be able to help the United States of America to go beyond survival.

Simon J. Ortiz
Deetseyamah
Spring 1991

Going for the Rain

PROLOGUE

There is a song which goes like this:

> Let us go again, brother; let us go for the shiwana.
> Let us make our prayer songs.
> We will go now. Now we are going.
> We will bring back the shiwana.
> They are coming now. Now, they are coming.
> It is flowing. The plants are growing.
> Let us go again, brother; let us go for the shiwana.

A man makes his prayers; he sings his songs. He considers all that is important and special to him, his home, children, his language, the self that he is. He must make spiritual and physical preparation before anything else. Only then does anything begin.

A man leaves; he encounters all manners of things. He has adventures, meets people, acquires knowledge, goes different places; he is always looking. Sometimes the traveling is hazardous; sometimes he finds meaning and sometimes he is destitute. But he continues; he must. His traveling is a prayer as well, and he must keep on.

A man returns, and even the returning has moments of despair and tragedy. But there is beauty and there is joy. At times he is confused, and at times he sees with utter clarity. It is all part of the traveling that is a prayer. There are things he must go through before he can bring back what he seeks, before he can return to himself.

The rain comes and falls. The shiwana have heeded the man, and they have come. The man has brought back the rain. It falls, and it is nourishing. The man returns to the strength that his selfhood is, his home, people, his language, the knowledge of who he is. The cycle has been traveled; life has beauty and meaning, and it will continue because life has no end.

THE FIRST: THE PREPARATION

The Creation, According to Coyote

"First of all, it's all true."
Coyote, he says this, this way,
humble yourself, motioning and meaning
what he says.

You were born when you came
from that body, the earth;
your black head burst from granite,
the ashes cooling,

until it began to rain.
It turned muddy then,
and then green and brown things
came without legs.

They looked strange.
Everything was strange.
There was nothing to know then,

until later, Coyote told me this,
and he was b.s.-ing probably,
two sons were born,
Uyuyayeh and Masaweh.
They were young then,
and then later on they were older.

And then the people were wondering
what was above.
They had heard rumors.

But, you know, Coyote,
he was mainly bragging
when he said (I think),
"My brothers, the Twins then said,
'Let's lead these poor creatures
and save them.'"

And later on, they came to light
after many exciting and colorful and tragic things
    of adventure;
and this is the life, all these, all these.

My uncle told me all this, that time.
Coyote told me too, but you know
how he is, always talking to the gods,
the mountains, the stone all around.

And you know, I believe him.

Forming Child

April 1973

IST ONE

O child's tremble
against your mother's innerwall,
is a true movement
without waste or hesitation,
a beating of wings
following ancient trails
to help us return.

2ND ONE

I will point
out your place on the earth,
among mountains, on ground,
by old watercourses, in wind,
where your mother walked,
where her mother walked.
This way then,
This way,
I will show you those points
where you will present yourself.

3RD ONE

Two days ago
when I was at the foot of Black Mountain,
there were rain clouds forming
in a space between the tip of the mountain
and a point in the sky.
Two days before that,
I saw a hawk circling
in a slow, cool wind
south of that place
where I stood watching.

4TH ONE

Years ago, your brother and I
walked from Chee Goodluck's hogan
in the Lukachukai Mountains
to a place where water
flowed from under huge granite boulders.
The water tasted like the wind,
roots, fresh herbs, sweet smells.

5TH ONE

I want you to see a pass
in the Chuska Mountains
where there are aspen, oak,
elevation high enough
for fir and snow
enough to last till June.
I've been up there twice,
once on a hard winter day.

6TH ONE

Among the things I would require
of you is that you should relish
the good wheat bread your mother makes,
taking care that you should think
how her hands move, kneading the dough,
shaping it with her concern,
and how you were formed and grew in her.

7TH ONE

Near the Summit, SE of Kinlichee,
I saw a piece of snowmelt water
that I thought would look good
on a silver bracelet with maybe
two small turquoise stones at its sides;
but then, I liked the way it was, too,
under pine trees, the snow feeding it,
the evening sunlight slanting off it,
and I knew that you would understand
why I decided to leave it like that.

8TH ONE

Yesterday, as I was lighting a cigarette,
Raho warned me with,
"If anyone starts a fire,
Smokey the Bear will come put them out."
Bear's got a lot of friends.

Four Poems for a Child Son

December 18, 1972

"WHAT'S YOUR INDIAN NAME?"

It has to do with full moments
of mountains, deserts, sun, gods,
song, completeness.

It has to do with stories, legends
full of heroes and traveling.

It has to do with rebirth and growing
and being strong and seeing.

You see it's like this (the movement):
go to the water
and gather the straight willow stems
bring them home
work carefully at forming them
tie on the feathers
paint them with the earth
feed them and talk with them
pray.

You see, son, the eagle is a whole person
the way it lives; it means it has to do
with paying attention to where it is,
not the center of the earth especially

but part of it, one part among all parts,
and that's only the beginning.

IT WAS THE THIRD DAY, JULY 12, 1971

Hitchhiking on the way to Colorado,
I heard your voice, "Look, Dad . . ."
                    A hawk
sweeping its wings
                        clear

through the whole sky

                    the blue
                    the slow wind
fresh with the smell of summer alfalfa
at the foot of the Jemez Mountains.

(You see, the gods come during the summer
for four days amongst the people,
bring gifts, bring hope and life,
you can see them, I mean.)

Waiting for my next ride,
I sang,
            Look, the plants with bells.
            Look, the stones with voices.

YESTERDAY

In the late afternoon,
there was suddenly a noise of birds
filling up everything.

This morning in the newspaper,
I read about starlings at the Air Force base.

I guess they were but all I knew yesterday
was that they filled up the trees,
the utility wires, the sky, the world.

That's all I know.

WHAT MY UNCLE TONY TOLD MY SISTER AND ME

Respect your mother and father.
Respect your brothers and sisters.
Respect your uncles and aunts.
Respect your land, the beginning.
Respect what is taught you.
Respect what you are named.
Respect the gods.
Respect yourself.
Everything that is around you
is part of you.

The Expectant Father

I am an expectant father.

Pray then:
smile for all good things,
note the wind,
note the rain,
touch the gentleness with care;
be good.

After we had watched the hawk circling in the hot wind and lost it
against the color of the mesa across the valley, we decided to climb
down the mesa to this spring. We walked for about half a mile and
finally arrived there. The spring is in a cave made by two huge slabs of
sandstone cliff leaning into each other. The water dripped from soft
crumbly shale and ran into a small pool. Around the water were hand-
high green ferny plants and moss grew on stone. There were move-
ments in the water which were our reflections and the tiny water
beings that lived there. Earl dipped into the water with a rusty can and
drank and then Gilly.

It was my turn then. The spring water tasted sweet and like a dark underground cavern, but something of a taste that was more like a touching wind than anything else. There was something else too, something else. We were quite young then. We weren't so tired and hot after a while anymore, and we climbed on down to the flat valley and looked somemore for our horses.

When the child comes, expectant father,
tell the child.
When I have awoken in the early mornings,
I have felt the child's flutter at the small of my back,
the mother's belly pressed against me.
The child is a butterfly cupped in the Mother's hands.
Be gentle, Naya; be kind, this morning
and for all mornings of our—your children's—lives.

When it rains in a soft wind,
it feels so good.

To Insure Survival

*for Rainy Dawn
born July 5, 1973*

You come forth
the color of a stone cliff
at dawn,
changing colors,
blue to red
to all the colors of the earth.

Grandmother Spider speaks
laughter and growing
and weaving things
and threading them
together to make life
to wear;
all these, all these.

You come out, child,
naked as that cliff at sunrise,
shorn of anything
except spots of your mother's blood.
You just kept blinking your eyes
and trying to catch your breath.

In five more days,
they will come,
singing, dancing,
bringing gifts,
the stones with voices,
the plants with bells.
They will come.

Child, they will come.

Language

> "The Word is sacred to a
> child."—N. Scott Momaday,
> House Made of Dawn

I carried my baby daughter to her bed,
laid her down; she turned her head aside,
and I patted her back, murmured a singsong,
and she fell asleep making small universal sounds.

Later she calls out—
from the next room—
go to pick her up—
she is so warm
a young animal—movement—

take her before the long
mirror—say Rainy, Rainy
murmur sound—she reaches
her hand—meets her own

hand—hand meets mirrored
hand—she smiles at my
mirrored face—what
does she think?

What is it, the murmur, the song of a chant,
drawn out holler, deep caress in the throat,
the wind searching hillside ledge?

The language of movements—sights—
possibilities and impossibilities—
pure existence—which leap into exact
moments—keep being there all the time—
static quality needing nothing else—
being its only validity—
adequate unto itself—solid—
to know it one has to become a part
of it—a word is the poem—child
upon hearing a sound hears the poem
of hearing—original motion of it
is complete—sanctified—the sphere
of who he or she is who is hearing
the poetry—motion of inwards a drawn
breath—complete entity of sound/word
has its own energy and motion.

Rainy sound is something like, "Uh oh"
motion of air, muscles,
tiny soft bones in upper chest,
mouth opening, moist cavern,
symbol of her beginning word,
pucker lips into,
"Where do sounds come from?"

From the deep well
where all points meet
and intercross again
and countless times
again.

The throat sound
knows its intercrossings;
the first sound,
it overflows and touches me.

She whispers another sound,
meaning,
"What is it? What shall I do
for you, child?"
comes from me, an extension
of herself.

I listened to the wind yesterday,
another sound. Travels
into me. Purpose: be simple
and thoughtful, flowing
with a singular pulsing.
All language comes forth
outward from the center. Hits
the curve of your being. Fits

    —"chiseled" occurs to me
      out of an unremembered passage
      in some book, has to do
      with image required to remember
      or remembered; "chiseled"
      into mind or memory stone—

into thoughts of sound itself,
the energy it is
and the motion inherent in it.

Four Bird Songs

FIRST SONG

Is a little wind
fledgling
nestled
in mountain's crooked finger,

is a river
into a secret place
that shows everything,
little song.

In your breath,
hold this seed
only a while
and seek with it.

One single universe,
I
am
only a little.

SECOND SONG

The sound
in wood,
a morning hollowness
of a cave on the flank of a small hill

startles
with its moan,
yearning,
a twitch of skin.

In the distant place,
a wind starts

coming here,
a waiting sound.

It is here now.
Shiver.
You are rewarded
for waiting.

THIRD SONG

By breathing he started
into the space
before him
and around him,

cleared his throat,
said this song
maybe tomorrow
is for rain.

Lightly
hummed
a tight leathersound
and then heavily.

It rained
the next day,
and he sang
another song for that.

FOURTH SONG

An old stone
was an old blue,
spotted,
the egg's shell,

only moments before
under the sun
that had become new
against old sand.

A tear falling,
stirring into space,
filling it completely,
making new space.

When he touched it,
and it moved,
it was still warm
with that life.

Time and Motion and Space

I told Barbara,
"When I was a kid
we used to throw rocks
off the cliffedges at Aacqu.
We were fascinated
because the falling of rock
seems to be something
like stopping time.

I mean it seems real
and clear to you then.
Time is so deep, fathomless,
and all the *time*
that you can't pin it down
at exact points nor with explanations.
But being witness to falling rock. . . .
Time is tangible then.
It is a rock falling
from the release of your hand,
moving into, through, down
space to the ground
at bottom cliffedge.
That's how you know then.

Time and motion and space:
pine and fir,
the wind,
lichen on sunwarm flat rock,
a road below in the valley,
voices of friends,
ourselves.
"Pine song," she said.
Butterfly comes by.
And then Bee all dressed
in bright yellow and black.

"This is the way it is."

"I'm not just making it up."

Buck Nez

*a birthday pup present for
me from friends; I was
taking him home for my son*

Ten miles
the other side of Nageezi,
we stopped
a mile south of the highway.

I built a fire big enough
to signal the gods.

You slept against my neck,
curled by my soul. Once,
I awoke to a tiny whimper,
and I worried
that I should feed you
when I had nothing to eat
myself.

55

It rained that night,
and it got cold.

In the morning,
I woke up to find
a puppy, you, yapping
like the original life,
a whole mystery crying
for sustenance.

We prayed.

What I want is a full life
for my son,
for myself,
for my Mother,
the Earth.

The Poet

"Are you really a poet?"

"Shore."

Crickets always talk like that.

A couple nights after,
I listened for a long time
to a couple reminding themselves
about 10 million years ago
in some cave in Asia.
It was a long, long time ago.
They rattled membranes together
and sang all night long.

"I didn't know you were a poet."

Later on,
there was another cave.
A woman was moaning,
and later she was laughing,
not very far from a glacier's edge.
To the south were swaying grasses,
brightly colored birds, warm oceans,
hot deserts, and strange gods
who demanded nothing.

She asked me if I liked crickets.
I said, "Yeah, but not cockroaches."
I wondered out loud
if cockroaches are any relation
to crickets, and she said, "Maybe,
but not too close."
I want to look it up somewhere,
but ten million years
is a hell of a long time
to really clear it up.

"How long you been a cricket?"

My Father's Song

Wanting to say things,
I miss my father tonight.
His voice, the slight catch,
the depth, from his thin chest,
the tremble of emotion
in something he has just said
to his Son, his song:

We planted corn one Spring at Aacqu—
we planted several times

but this one particular time
I remember the soft damp sand
in my hand.

My father had stopped at one point
to show me an overturned furrow;
the plowshare had unearthed
the burrow nest of a mouse
in the soft moist sand.

Very gently, he scooped tiny pink animals
into the palm of his hand
and told me to touch them.
We took them to the edge
of the field and put them in the shade
of a sand moist clod.

I remember the very softness
of cool and warm sand and tiny alive
mice and my father saying things.

Two Women

She is a Navajo woman sitting at her loom.
The sun is not far up,
but she has already prepared
her husband's and sons' breakfasts,
and they have eaten and left.
Today, her husband will pull the weeds
from among the pumpkin, squash, and cornplants
in their small field at the mouth of Redwater Wash.
The two sons have driven their sheep and goats
to the Hill With White Stones. And she is left
in the calm of her work at the loom.

Quickly, Grandmother,
the Spider spins,
quick flips and turns,
the colors.

O the colors, Grandmother,
I saw in the two-days-ago rainbow.

O Grandmother Spider, the sun is shining
through your loom.

She works gently, her skirt flared out,
in the sun of this morning's Summer.

Desbah is grinding corn into meal.
The kernels of the corn are blue
with a small scattering of whites;
they are hard and she can hear them
crack sharply under the handstone
she is using. She reaches into a sack
for the corn and puts them on the stone.
Her father, Silversmith, brought it
one evening to her. He had it tied
on his horse with some rope,
and it was wrapped in some canvas cloth.

As she stops momentarily grinding,
she can hear him again say, "This stone
for the grinding of corn is for my child.
The man who gets her will be pleased,
but he will not like to carry this heavy thing
around," and he had laughed with his love
and hopes for her. Silversmith had gone
on ahead many years ago, and she never did
have a man get her.

She can hear the blue and white kernels
crack sharply on the heavy stone.

Poem for Jody About Leaving

I was telling you
about the red cliff faces
of the Lukachukai Mountains—
how it is
going away—
and near Tsegi,
the red and brown land
that is like a strong
and healthy woman
ready to give birth
to many children,
and you don't ever want to go
but do anyway.

THE SECOND: LEAVING

Toward Spider Springs

I was amazed
at the wall of stones
by the roadside.

Our baby, his mother,
and I were trying to find
the right road,
but all we found
were ones deeply rutted
and high centered.
We were trying to find
a place to start all over
but couldn't.

On the way back,
we passed by
the stone walls again.
The stones had no mortar;
they were just stones
balancing against the sky.

Arrival in Sudden Seaside
Fog This Morning

Last night traveling
through the barebone desert
parts of Arizona and California,
a variety of discomforts
riding my poor body
through the long-distance night
of Casa Grande, Dateland,
Yuma, El Centro, and now
this morning early,
they have become roadside ghosts
vanished into the sudden fog.

Blues Song for the Phoenix Bus
Depot Derelict

Waiting for my bus
that comes in tonight
then leaves me
sitting here.
Waiting to leave.
Waiting to come.
Please,
I know Phoenix streets
cold gray and hard.
Please,
leave me alone
for tonight.
Sitting here coming and going,

I'm waiting for everything
to arrive
just this one time for me.

Many Farms Notes

taken on a Many Farms,
Arizona, trip, Spring 1973

1
Hawk circles
on wind roads
only he knows
how to follow
to the center.

2
Hawk's bright eyes
read trees, stones,
points in horizon,
movements, how wind
and shadows play
tricks, and sudden
rabbit flurry
which reminds him
of his empty stomach.

3
A Tuba City girl asks me
if I ever write from paintings.
I tell her that I write
with visions in my head.

4
I'm walking out of Gallup.
He calls, "Hey, my fren,
where you going too fas'?"

"Many Farms."
"Good lucks."
I smile for his good thoughts.

5
A wind vision:
if you look into the Chinle Valley,
you will see the Woman's cover,
a tapestry her Old Mother worked
for 10 million years or so.

6
On the way south to the junction,
I looked to the northeast
and couldn't decide whether that point
in the distance beyond the Defiance uplift
was Sonsela Butte or Fluted Rock.

7
The L.A. Kid was a city child
and a Navajo rodeo queen,
who said she'd seen me on the road
coming out of Window Rock,
said her friend had said,
"I think that was him;
we just passed him up,"
and felt so bad,
said she was born in L.A.
but wasn't really a city girl
and visited her homeland
every Summer, and said
her mother was from Lukachukai.

8
Bear occurs several times, of course:

The day before I went to Many Farms,
received a card from Snyder,
said he'd "spent a day watching grizzly bear"
grizzling at the San Diego Zoo.

Navajo girl had a painting of Bear.
He was facing east and looking up.
A line was drawn through him,
from chest to tail, rainbow muted colors,
and I said, "That line seems to be both
the horizon and the groundline where you start."

She told me what the people say.
Don't ever whistle at night where bears are,
because female bears do that
when there are courting bears around.
Remember that: don't whistle
in the dark, horny Bear night.

That Navajo girl asked me
what I thought about polygamy.
I told her I thought it was a good idea
but not for keeps, and we laughed.
I wonder how many wives Bear has?

9
For Monday night supper, we had
mutton ribs, round steak,
good Isleta bread, tortillas,
broccoli, green chili, potatoes,
gravy, coffee, and apple pie.
The mutton was tough and Francis said,
"You gotta be tough
to live on this land."

10
After I got out of the back
of a red pickup truck,
I walked for about a mile
and met three goats, two sheep and a lamb
by the side of the road.
I was wearing a bright red wool cap
pulled over my ears,
and I suppose they thought I was maybe weird

because they were all ears and eyes.
I said, "Yaahteh, my friends.
I'm from Acoma, just passing through."
The goat with the bell jingled it
in greeting a couple of times.
I could almost hear the elder sheep
telling the younger, "You don't see many
Acoma poets passing through here."

11
"What would you say that the main theme
of your poetry is?"
"To put it as simply as possible,
I say it this way: to recognize
the relationships I share with everything."

I would like to know well the path
from just east of Black Mountain
to the gray outcropping of Roof Butte
without having to worry
about the shortest way possible.

12
I worried about two women discussing how
to get rid of a Forming Child
without too much trouble, whether
it would be in the hospital in Gallup
or in Ganado.
Please forgive my worry and my concern.

13
"Are you going to Gallup, shima?"
"Yes."
"One dollar and fifty cents, please."

Old Hills

West of Ocotillo Wells,
the hills are pretty old.
In fact, they're older than any signs
telling tourists where they're at,
older than all of millennium's signpainters.

I was there with a number
of university students.
They were making a film
in the desert about an old Indian
who was burying his daughter,
planting her back into the earth.

The completed film, in color,
worth six semester credit hours,
was about life. The director
was a young Crow man
who had grown up in Los Angeles.

The rocks and cacti tolerate us
very quietly; they probably laugh
softly at us with the subtle chuckle
of ancient humor that our jubilant youth
knows not yet to recognize and share.

Beane, a Black youth from Watts,
was adjusting a light meter,
and he had trouble with some figures,
and Doug, the Crow from L.A.,
hollered, "Beane, I don't think you understand
what the hell the sun has to do with your shadow."

These hills are pretty old.
Some have worn down to flat desert valley.
Some stones remember being underwater
and the cool fresh green winds.

21 August '71 Indian

Building the fire,
using shavings I made this afternoon
as I attempted a sculpture, a bird
or the wisp of high thin cloud in Fall,
from a length of curved white pine.
The fire is slow to catch,
wood is damp, but it begins to start,
and I throw on the larger pieces.

An old girlfriend came by a while ago,
fat and getting older,
wearing wide dark glasses;
she held a fat and healthy baby.
I was making tortillas then,
flour on my hands, rolling dough out
on a board with a tall drinking glass.
She didn't say anything
as her husband and I talked;
I was glad she didn't ask why
I was not a lawyer or an engineer.

Fire burns the thin shavings quickly
and soon dies down under larger pieces.
The red coals are weak, have to watch
and put smaller pieces on next time.
Get knife and splinter larger into smaller
and feed the coals, being patient.
Will have a late supper tonight;
maybe the clouds will part some by then
and let me see some stars.

It's been years since.
I told her then of the things
I was discovering about myself.
I took long evening walks
and listened to the sounds of rivers,
and she would come looking for me.

She never knew, I don't think, until today
that I could make tortillas—
that I've learned to survive this way—
over a fire for my lone supper.

Fire burns good now, good red coals.
Will get the beans and tortillas
to warm over the glowing coals.
I will have purple plums for dessert.
I am able to see some stars now, too.
I don't think I'll ever be an engineer
or at least even a lawyer.

Hesperus Acoma
Summer 1971

Small Things Today

at my Hesperus Camp

Had a tortilla with some honey
at midafternoon. It was good.
Wished I had some chili.

Smell of apples, wet fields;
in back of the blue tent
is a box of last season's
Animas Valley apples; soon,
it will be another Fall.

Wind blows, shakes the tarp,
water falls to the ground.
The sound of water splashing.

Several hours ago, watched
a woodpecker watching me.
We both moved our heads
with funny jerks.

Rex and his sad, dog eyes.

Somebody looking around in a field,
looking for lost things.

Notice bean sprouts growing.
They're very pale and nude.

Rex doesn't like chicken livers,
but gizzards are okay.

Travels in the South

I. EAST TEXAS

When I left the Alabama–Coushatta people,
it was early morning.
They had treated me kindly, given me food,
spoken me words of welcome, and thanked me.
I touched them, their hands, and promised
I would be back.

When I passed by the Huntsville State Pen
I told the Indian prisoners what the people said
and thanked them and felt very humble.
The sun was rising then.

When I got to Dallas I did not want to be there.
I went to see the BIA Relocation man.
He told me, "I don't know how many Indians
there are in Dallas; they come every week."
I talked with Ray, a Navajo; he didn't have a job,
was looking, and he was a welder.
I saw an Apache woman crying for her lost life.

When it was evening of the next day,
I stopped at a lake called Caddo.
I asked a park ranger, "Who was Caddo?"
And he said it used to be some Indian tribe.

I met two Black women fishing at the lake.
I sat by them; they were good to be with.
They were about seventy years old and laughed,
and for the first and only time in my life
I cut a terrapin's head off because,
as the women said, "They won't let go until sundown."

When it was after sundown in East Texas, I prayed
for strength and the Caddo and the Black women
and my young son at home and Dallas and when
it would be the morning, the Sun.

2. THE CREEK NATION EAST OF THE MISSISSIPPI

Once, in a story, I wrote that Indians are everywhere.
Goddamn right.

In Pensacola, Florida, some hotdog stand
operator told me about Chief McGee.

"I'm looking for Indians," I said.
"I know Chief Alvin McGee," he said.
I bought a hotdog and a beer.
"He lives near Atmore, Alabama,
cross the tracks, drive by the school,
over the freeway to Atlanta, about a mile.
He lives at the second house on the right."

I called from a payphone in Atmore.
Mr. McGee told me to come on over.
I found his home right away,
and he came out when I stopped in his yard.
He had a big smile on his face.
I'd seen his face before in the history books
when they bothered to put Creeks in them.

73

He told me about Osceola.
"He was born in this county," Chief McGee said.
He showed me his garden and fields.
"I have seventy acres," he said.
"We used to have our own school,
but they took that away from us.
There ain't much they don't try to take."

We watched the news on TV.
It was election time in Alabama,
George Wallace against something.
People kept coming over to his house,
wanting the Chief's support. "Wallace is the one."
"Brewer is our man." They kept that up all night.
The next morning the election was on,
but I left right after breakfast.

Chief Alvin McGee put his arms around me
and blessed me. I remembered my grandfather,
the mountains, the land from where I came,
and I thanked him for his home, "Keep together,
please don't worry about Wallace, don't worry."

I was on that freeway to Atlanta
when I heard about the killings at Kent State.
I pulled off the road just past a sign which read
NO STOPPING EXCEPT IN CASE OF EMERGENCY
and hugged a tree.

3. CROSSING THE GEORGIA BORDER INTO FLORIDA

I worried about my hair, kept my car locked.
They'd look at me, lean, white, nervous,
their lips moving, making wordless gestures.

My hair is past my ears.
My Grandfather wore it like that.
He used to wear a hat, a gray one,
with grease stains on it.
The people called him Tall One

because he was tall for an Acoma.

I had a hard time in Atlanta;
I thought it was because
I did not have a suit and tie.
I had to stay at the Dinkler Plaza,
a classy joint, for an Indian meeting.
The desk clerk didn't believe it
when I walked up, requested a room,
towel rolled up under my arm,
a couple books, and my black bag of poems.
I had to tell him who I really wasn't.
He charged me twenty dollars for a room,
and I figured I'm sure glad
that I'm not a Black man,
and I was sure happy to leave Atlanta.

A few miles from the Florida line,
I picked some flowers beside the highway
and put them with the sage I got in Arizona.
After the Florida line, I went to a State Park,
paid two-fifty, and the park ranger told me,
"This place is noted for the Indians
that don't live here anymore."
He didn't know who they used to be.

When I got to my campsite
and lay on the ground,
a squirrel came by and looked at me.
I moved my eyes. He moved his head.
"Brother," I said.
A red bird came, hopped.
"Brother, how are you?" I asked.
I took some bread, white, and kind of stale,
and scattered some crumbs before them.
They didn't take the crumbs,
and I didn't blame them.

Relocation

Don't talk me no words.
Don't frighten me
for I am in the blinding city.
The lights,
the cars,
the deadened glares
    tear my heart
    and close my mind.

Who questions my pain,
the tight knot of anger
in my breast?

I swallow hard and often
and taste my spit
and it does not taste good.
Who questions my mind?

I came here because I was tired;
the BIA taught me to cleanse myself,
daily to keep a careful account of my time.
Efficiency was learned in catechism;
the nuns spelled me God in white.
And I came here to feed myself—
corn, potatoes, chili, and mutton
did not nourish me they said.

So I agreed to move.
I see me walking in sleep
down streets, down streets gray with cement
and glaring glass and oily wind,
armed with a pint of wine,
I cheated my children to buy.
I am ashamed.
I am tired.
I am hungry.

I speak words.
I am lonely for hills.
I am lonely for myself.

Busride Conversation

She says,
"I came to Albuquerque
on Wednesday."

She's about eighteen.

"I have three shell necklaces
ready to sell.
A man offered me thirty dollars."

She smells slightly sour
with sweat, the several nights
in Albuquerque.

We mention names
to each other,
people we know,
places we've been.

She says, "In May,
I was in Gallup jail
with a girl from Acoma."

I've been there too.

"The cook was an Apache.
He sneaked two chiliburgers
in to us.
He was sure good to us."

She giggles, and I laugh.
She gets off at Domingo Junction.

"Be good," I say.

"You too," she says.

Portrait of a Poet
with a Console TV
in Hand

I bought that TV at John's TV
on College Avenue in San Diego
and lugged it all the way home
on the Greyhound bus.

Sitting in Phoenix bus depot
waiting room, TV sitting on my lap,
I felt foolish as I watched
depot officials grab an old man
derelict as he searched dazedly
into an open locker compartment.
They pushed him reeling out
into deadly stunning American city.
At 12:30 A.M., there wasn't anything else on,
just that already too late, late channel.

I had known that I would be coming home
but the TV-in-hand bit
was an entirely new angle, and I think
that it must have to do with an odd madness.

Surprise

On Friday we passed
through mountains,
through place called Alpine,
handlettered signs
on apple cider roadside stands,
a small lake, lots of pine
and higher up twisted aspen
made me lonesome for Crystal
on Arizona–New Mexico line.

Yesterday, it snowed
only seventy miles southeast
of San Diego in the Cuyamac Mtns.
Monday morning, I am very clear
in my head—realize
I didn't get drunk all weekend.
Surprises, I like to learn
from them when I'm clear.

Early Morning

One knows
some instinctive response
to movements.
Shadowed murmurs,
softly, softly
go away.
The faintest quiver

at the edge
of awakedness.
Quiet, child,
my soul—
don't move now,
not yet.
Wait just a while.

I heard streetsweepers
at least three times
early this morning.
Now, I wonder
if they were
only occurrences
in my dreams.

The other times
there was more silence
than I have ever felt
in the streets before.
Acres and acres
of silence.

Where was the moon?

Making an Acquaintance

I walk outside without my shoes
on searing hot asphalt front yard.
Howard, my new landlord, says,
"It's gonna be a bitch of a Summer."
Strange, I think, what words mean.
He has a tanned middle-aged face,
used to be in real estate in Ohio,

sold his business and moved West.
We get acquainted by talking
about the coming Summer.
"Yeah," I agree with him,
"it's gonna be a bitch."
My feet are burning for coolness.

Without You

What to do without you
is night madness.

Once you called up,
"I was crossing the street
and suddenly there was nothing
around me."

There is nothing around you.
You are an island.
The ocean is overbrimmed.
Sometimes it is too late
for anything else.

You said,
"I'll try to make it home,
but there's all that traffic."

"Okay," I said,
and I watched for you
and finally saw
your shadowed figure
come swimming homeward.

The Poems I Have Lost

She said to take the L-Train
to . . . .

I know where I left them—
on the floor of her apartment
with five locks on Thirteenth Street,
Somewhere Else City, USA.
I don't think I'll ever go back.

A young couple picked me up
east miles out of Asheville—
had just started a poem too—
and we stopped and smoked
at a roadside table
at the edge of June tobacco fields.
I lost them somewhere
between there and the Atlantic Ocean.

I wrote Duffie a long rambling
letter, called it a poem,
from Nashville, because
I got lonesome for sunsets
in Colorado Springtime and then
dropped the letter in the mailbox.
I wonder if it ever found her in Juneau, Alaska.

The last thing I remember
was leaning into the roots
of a piñon tree. It wasn't
the horse that had thrown me;
it wasn't McCallister either
who owned the horse. It was
all that damn beer we had
been drinking all afternoon.

I got a letter from St. Paul, Minn.
inviting me up there to read poems.

I fell off the plane in Denver,
lost my ticket and most of my poems
but managed to hold on enough
to a few remaining things.

Memories, I guess they are,
crowd me because of all the signals
I've missed, the poems that keep
coming back in pieces.

Fragments remain with me, of course;
I touch the bare skeletons, smell
the old things, and see new visages pass
many, many times.
These are enough.

How Close

I wonder if I have ever come close
to seeing the first seed, the origin,
and where?

I've thought about it, says Coyote.

Once I thought I saw it in the glint
of a mica stratum a hairwidth deep.
I was a child then,
cradled in my mother's arm.
We were digging for the gray clay
to make pottery with.

That was south of Acoma years back;
that was the closest I've gotten yet.

I've thought about it, says Coyote.

Last Night

New York City almost got me
last night at Kennedy Airport.
So messed up,
making phone calls to places
I can't even remember.

Just held on tight
to my bag of poems, my life,
fighting off sleep,
the moments that can swallow you
without your knowledge of where
you are disappearing to.

Finally, got a cab,
finally, got to a friend's place.
A phone call to you then,
lay on a carpet,
ate couple good apples,
drank glass of bourbon,
and it was already morning.
But, finally, I got to talk to you.
It was good, that part,
and I went to sleep on the floor
beside the phone and two apple cores.

Today, the A-Train, 168th to 14th

. . . The A-Train shakes bad
for this Indian.
I see blank faces, an old woman, a Black man,
somebody clutching a bag for her life.
I watch the numbers flashing by,
one blackness thunders into another,
another train crashes by headed uptown.
I can't even recognize anybody.

It is a relief to get off, and I walk,
trying to judge by the vague sun
which way I'm going, and I watch some construction
going on. I think of arbitration or something
like that, cross several streets and look
for the time, trying to make it meaningful.
I had even forgotten when it was
I was supposed to meet you.

Hunger in New York City

Hunger crawls into you
from somewhere out of your muscles
or the concrete or the land
or the wind pushing you.

It comes to you, asking
for food, words, wisdom, young memories
of places you ate at, drank cold spring water,
or held somebody's hand,

or home of the gentle, slow dances,
the songs, the strong gods, the world
you know.

That is, hunger searches you out.
It always asks you,
How are you, son? Where are you?
Have you eaten well?
Have you done what you as a person
of our people is supposed to do?

And the concrete of this city,
the oily wind, the blazing windows,
the shrieks of automation cannot,
truly cannot, answer for that hunger
although I have hungered,
truthfully and honestly, for them
to feed myself with.

So I sang to myself quietly:
I am feeding myself
with the humble presence
of all around me;
I am feeding myself
with your soul, my mother earth;
make me cool and humble.
Bless me.

Traveled All the Way
to New York City

How are you?
Fine, and you?

It was good to touch you.

I liked your floppy black hat,

I liked that place we went to.
You had three beers,
I had three beers—
if I remember correctly.

I forgot to give you some sage
I had brought in a plastic bag.
I picked it in Arizona.
Next time, I'll remember.

That delicatessen was wild,
a real Jewish gourmet disneyland,
and I was like a little boy.
I could have stayed a long time.

You live in a nice place
even though you need five locks.

What was your cat's name?

Later, I said—an old line—
"I traveled all the way to New York
just to see you." Aaaiiieee!

Laughing, it's so good to laugh.

—Indian 1970 in NYC

87

For Those Sisters & Brothers in Gallup

He is that twisted shadow
under the bridge: he is
that broken root.
I know where he came from: I've
known you for so long
I want to take you home.

He got hit outside the city limits:
once
I saw a scatter of flesh and blood
mashed into the highway
east of Gallup.
                The car wheels
shuddered over a lump,
and my body and soul shud-
dered, o my god.
                I turned
around up the road and drove
slowly back,
                o my god.
It was a dog left in tatters
of skin, splintered bone,
blood, and I dragged raggy meat
which was the leg and threw it
as hard
                and as far as I could
away from the Interstate
and prayed and moaned for us.

O my god, I know what is my name:
she stumbled like a stuffed dummy
against me, looked into my mouth
with her opaque remorseful eyes
and asked me for a drink.

I HAVE DRUNK AND TRIED TO KILL
MY ANGER IN YOUR GODDAMNED TOWN
AND I'M AFRAID FOR YOU AND ME
WHEN I WILL COME BACK AGAIN.

Be kind, sister, be kind;
it shall come cleansing again.
It shall rain and your eyes
will shine and look so deeply
into me into me into me into me.

Evening Beach Walk

I don't really feel like walking
at first
but somehow feel I must
since I have come
this far
to this edge,
and so I walk.

The sun is going downwards
or rather one point changes to another,
and I know I am confronting
another horizon.

A dog comes sniffing at my knees
and I hold my hand to him,
and he sniffs, wags his tail
and trots away to join a young couple,
his friends, who smile as we meet.

I look many times as the sun sets
and I don't know why I can't see

clearly the horizon that I've imagined.
Maybe it's the clouds, the smog,
maybe it's the changing.

It's a duty with me,
I know, to find the horizons,
and I keep on walking on the ocean's edge,
looking for things in the dim light.

A Patience Poem for the Child That Is Me

Be patient child,
be patient, quiet.
The rivers run into the center
of the earth
and around
revolve all things
and flow
into the center.
Be patient, child,
quiet.

THE THIRD: RETURNING

The Wisconsin Horse

*It is late at night, lying
drunk on the floor, hearing
a church bell across the
street, remembering that
Wisconsin Horse
this Spring.*

One step at a time to return.

The horse across the road
stands within a fence,
silent in the hot afternoon.

A mile north is some construction.
I tell the horse,
"That's America building something."

A mile further through a clump of trees
is a river.

The Wisconsin Horse is silent.

The bell clamors
against the insides of my skull.
It has nothing to do with sound
that can comfort.

The clamor wants to escape
its barriers.
I want it to escape.
I have no defenses.

I should be an eager Christian
hungry for salvation,
or at the very least accept smugness
bound tightly in plastic.

Yet, at this single point in my life,
I know only a few bare things:
the floor, the walls around me,
that bell across the street,
that despair is a miserable excuse for emptiness,
that I should echo louder
that call for salvation
which at this point I know
is a need to fill the hollows
and pockets of my body.

Despair is such a poor excuse
to exclude things from my life,
to allow them to slip
from safe places.

    But now, and not too soon,
in, this dark night,
having gotten up to write,
I make this offering:
that Wisconsin Horse I saw
standing in the hot afternoon,
staring through a chainlink fence
at the construction going on
only a mile away,
I wonder now if the horse still stands
silent in the dark night,
dreamless and stifled,
having no recourses left
except to hope his silence
will soon go away
and the meaningfulness enter.

A Barroom Fragment

He was talking,
"I invited her to Las Vegas,
and when we got to the hotel
she asked for a separate room.
I told her, 'Shit, if you
want a room to yourself, why baby
that's alright, have it.'
I had brought her up there
on a four-million-dollar airplane,
and I told her, 'You can
go across the street
and take a thirty-thousand-dollar bus
back to Burbank.'"
That was Coyote talking.

Four Years Ago

Four years ago
I was in Wisconsin
somewhere,
making for the stateline,
crossing,
heading homewards.
I wondered
in what period of history
I was then.

I wonder that now.

Yesterday,
I told my wife,

"You must see me
in the perspective
of my whole life."

It all adds
ups and downs.

Horizons and Rains

Interstate 40 from Albuquerque
to Gallup—
witness to the brown people
stumbling Sunday afternoon
northwards—

   "Where's the rain that feels so good?"

and to Tsaile, the mountains, dark buttes—

"Maybe if the Hopis and Navajos
quit messing around," Ackley says.

   "Where it has always been."

The brown people losing trails
and finding trails and losing them
and finding again—

the horizons
and rains
in the far distance.

Leaving America

That time in Kansas City bus depot,
met Roy.

"Yaahteh, shikis."
"Where you from?"
"Arizona."
"Where you coming from?"
"Moline."

Jus' got paid,
laid off by the Rock Island Line.

Going home.
It's got red and brown land,
sage, and when it rains,
it smells like piñon
and pretty girls at a Squaw Dance.

I know.

Washyuma Motor Hotel

Beneath the cement foundations
of the motel, the ancient spirits
of the people conspire sacred tricks.
They tell stories and jokes and laugh
and laugh.

The American passersby
get out of their hot, stuffy cars
at evening, pay their money wordlessly,
and fall asleep without benefit of dreams.

The next morning, they get up,
dress automatically, brush their teeth,
get in their cars and drive away.
They haven't noticed that the cement
foundations of the motor hotel
are crumbling, bit by bit.

The ancient spirits tell stories
and jokes and laugh and laugh.

Passing Through Little Rock

The old Indian ghosts—
                    "Quapaw"
"Waccamaw"—
                    are just billboard words
in this crummy town.

"You know, I'm worrying a lot lately,"
he says in the old hotel bar.

"You're getting older and scared ain't you?"

I just want to cross the next hill,
go through that clump of trees
and come out the other side

and see a clean river,
the whole earth new
and hear the noise it makes
at birth.

Sometimes It's Better to Laugh
"Honest Injun"

Chicago O'Hare Field

You're Indian aren't you? this slim man
with a weak face asks me in a conspiring voice.
Yes, I nod. And he shows me a belt buckle.
Handmade, he tells me, but someone told me
that it was phony turquoise
and plastic records, junk.

I look at it, and it is plastic,
paste turquoise and shiny aluminum,
and I tell him, You may be right,
you know that?

You can't trust anybody these days,
he says.
And he gets sullen, says,
Got it in Flagstaff, know a lot of Indians
and I even know some in Wyoming.
They told me this was genuine, handmade,
but you can't trust anybody these days,
not even an honest injun.

He shows me a business card,
looks around with his shallow eyes.
It reads: Jackson Arms Corp.
       Jim Penning, Pres.
       Jackson Hole, Wyoming
He tells me in a low voice, I'm working
on a high frequency sound machine,
above human hearing. You ought to see
the way it works; it's neat.
It can really destroy things,
blow them apart just like that.
The laser ain't nothing. I'm working on it,
he reassures me. I nod my head,
but I'm not reassured, and I don't really
want to see the way it works, neatly.

99

I continue to drink my beer,
wondering about this weak-faced man
who is conspiring with me,
telling me his horrible secret,
this man whom an Indian sold a piece
of junk jewelry. Maybe that's why
he's pissed off and he's working
on a weapon to recoup his foolish purchase
and by his revelation to include me
in his conscience.

I ask him, Why? then. His eyes turn cloudy,
and he mumbles into his drink.
He doesn't know perhaps,
and he doesn't want to conspire
with me anymore, fearing
I will sell him
another piece of "genuine" jewelry.

I finish my beer, take a look
at O'Hare TV schedule monitors,
checking for departure announcement
but it's not there yet, and I walk
anyway into the concourse tunnel
for Gate 11-B and decide to laugh
my deep relief. And it's all true.

Missing That Indian Name of Roy or Ray

1
Can't even remember his name.
Maybe it was Roy or Ray—
tell Leslie that.
Drinking on Des Moines–to–K.C. bus,

throbbing with dull nerves,
going home, coming home,
talk to nobody until K.C. depot.
He's wobbling down from Chicago bus
first I see him.
"Yaahteh, where you from?"
"Sanders."
I know where Sanders is,
west of Gallup right off U.S. 66.
Roy, Navajo, coming from places.
New levis, new shirt, new everything,
just got laid off the Rock Island Line.
Right in style, man, don't talk English
too good, but that's okay,
expensive transistor radio we listen to.
That's okay, shikis,
I like cowboy music, sentimental crap,
go to dances at Milan's in Gallup,
saw somebody getting laid out in back once,
saw somebody get knifed there too.
Red blood black and shiny in neon light,
quick footsteps running away,
me and my buddy careful to approach him,
don't touch him, and then make a phone call.

In Kansas City bus depot,
two Indians going for a drink.
Wink at barmaid, two whiskies, two beers
settle down warm but in a hurry.
Look for danger.

Later on in the bus, he sings Navajo songs.
Indians singing, you sing
when there's a crowd, girls,
and fires that smell good.
　"Give me two dollars.
　　And I will like you."
A Black guy and a hippie girl
come and join us in the back.
　"No more dollar.
　　No more dollar."

In the early morning,
when it's getting light,
we're outside of Tulsa, and you see
those oil wells, pumping the juice,
nodding all the time, up and down,
up and down, all day, getting rich.
On the outskirts, we see a sign:
TULSA SCREW PRODUCTS, CO.,
and we laugh and laugh.

2
He gets lost in Amarillo.
Went to get a couple hamburgers
and then didn't show back up.
"Where's that Indian that was back here?"
the bus driver asks.
"Went to get some hamburgers," I tell him,
and then I run around the block
but can't find him;
at least he took his expensive radio with him.
Me and the Black guy and the hippie girl
keep looking out the back window
when we pull out of Amarillo.

3
The Black guy gets off in Tucumcari,
and I wonder that it's a strange place
for a Black man to get off at,
Tucumcari, New Mexico.

4
When I get off in Albuquerque,
the girl stays on.
"See you in Portland," she says.
And I walk up the street
missing that Indian we left behind
in Amarillo.

Crossing the Colorado River
into Yuma

It is almost dusk.

For a long time,
we've been traveling.

I saw a hawk
flying low against the sky.
The horizon was stone.

That was only a while back.

No one owns this river. Wash with it. Drink it.
Water your plants with it. Pray with it.

The evening sun glimmers across the desert.

Colors signal memories
of past journeys.

Sounds filled everything
and overflowed
upon returning.

Now, the river is silent.

The Greyhound bus roars smoothly on the bridge.
The river bed is hot sand.
The willows are last weak vestiges.
Alongside the river bed is a concrete canal.
The liquid in it flows swiftly, directed, and lifeless.

A brown man leans
by the Yuma bus depot wall;
a daze is in his eyes.

He tries and tries
to smell the river.

He leans,
trying to feel welcomed
to his home.

Yuma is a small town.
It abounds with modern Americana,
motels, gas stations, schools, churches, and etc.
Where did they all come from?
Do they really plan for survival this way?

Neon is weak.

Concrete will soon return
to desert.

Be patient, child, be kind
and not bitter.

Prepare for the morning.
Go down to the river bed.
It will let you.

Sing a bit, be patient.
Wait.

Valley of the Sun

Where's the Sun that feels so good?

Tired, nauseous in belly, breathe
the sandy wind at a roadside stop near Phoenix.
My son whimpers.
                    We traveled
from the Grand Canyon where we had awoken,
down through Prescott early in the morning
of Christmas Day. Nobody seemed awake;
it was a calm and deserted town.

I searched for a road to Skull Valley
where I'd spent one year of a boyhood.
Down through the mountains, a winding road,
recognized places where I learned to smoke,
consider enticing thoughts, to read,
explored, and where I'd almost gotten laid
on a hillside in a barn, an old musty barn
with useless hay. Later, I climbed down
into the sunlight, that knowledge trembling
in my mind, a boy growing for manhood.

Where's the Sun that feels so good?

A dim sun led us into Phoenix, the Valley
of the Sun, passed by John Jacob's Farm
where the lettuce grows
in such sterile lines.
They are taking the water with machines
out of the river, in fact, setting the course
of rivers, and they make artificial rain.

The
    sunlight
        is so
           dim,
passing by John Jacob's Farm.
We look for life. Look, but there are only lines
of lettuce converging at the far end.

Where's the Sun that feels so good?

There are stories about Montezuma.
He came from the south, a magnificent man,
a warrior, a saint, generous and gentle.
He carried a golden cane, they say,
and touching earth, green things would spring up,
and he led animals and people to water
he tapped out of solid stone.
There are these stories.

A Dying Warrior

Leonard Bluebird,
she tells me in Smitty's Bar,
sobbing immense sorrow,
is dying of leukemia.
I can't do nothing for him.
Look, he's limping.

The dying Leonard is wobbling
across the floor, dancing, drunk.
The music is crude and loud
and cowboy.
Many Indians staring.

O I can't look, she says.
He's got a sister,
but she can't do anything.
I'm the same way.
He doesn't want to die
in the Indian Hospital.

I step out into the night
concrete cliffed Phoenix,
sad and walking, cussing
at the streets and the dying bird.

I Told You I Like Indians

You meet Indians everywhere.

Once, I walked into this place—
Flagler Beach, Florida,
you'd never expect it—
a bar; some old people ran it.

The usual question, of course,
"You're an Indian, aren't you?"
"Yes, ma'am." I'm Indian alright.
Wild, ignorant, savage!
And she wants me to dance.
Well, okay, been drinking beer
all the way from Hollywood.
We dance something.

You're Indian aren't you?
Yeah, jeesus christ almighty,
I'm one of them.

I like Indians!

"There's an Indian around here."
What? And in walks a big Sioux.
Crissake man, how's relocation, brother?
He shakes my hand. Glad to see you.
I thought I was somewhere else.
We play the pingpong machine, drink beer,
once in a while dance with the old lady
who likes Indians.

I like Indians!

I *told* you
You meet Indians everywhere.

The Significance of a Veteran's Day

I happen to be a veteran
but you can't tell in how many ways
unless I tell you.

A cold morning waking up on concrete;
I never knew that feeling before,
calling for significance,
and no one answered.

Let me explain it this way
so that you may not go away
without knowing a part of me:

that I am a veteran of at least 30,000 years
when I traveled with the monumental yearning
of glaciers, relieving myself by them,
growing, my children seeking shelter
by the roots of pines and mountains.

When it was that time to build,
my grandfather said, "We cut stone and mixed mud
and ate beans and squash and sang
while we moved ourselves. That's what we did."
And I believe him.

And then later on in the ancient and deep story
of all our nights, we contemplated,
contemplated not the completion of our age,
but the continuance of the universe,
the traveling, not the progress,
but the humility of our being here.

Caught now, in the midst of wars
against foreign disease, missionaries,
canned food, Dick & Jane textbooks, IBM cards,
Western philosophies, General Electric,
I am talking about how we have been able
to survive insignificance.

To & Fro

On the train to California,
a Black porter told me,
"We don't serve Indians hard liquor, chief."
I said, "That's okay, man."
When I got home my wife asked,
"What are you doing back here?"
I said, "I came home."

Actually, I was a fugitive.
I had decided that at 8:00 A.M.
in the East Commons
over scalding coffee, sitting
at an imitation-wood table
as I watched crowds of students
mangle each other before breakfast.

I had several strange moments
thinking of Charles Olson
and language, thinking about a point
in particular the night before
when the night and the connections
were one and the same,
and I had touched a sustaining motion,
realizing the energy that language is
and becomes.

I had to leave California
I told my wife later
but kept secret that dove I heard
one precarious morning
when I was sick and moaned for home,
pushing back the memory of a boy
in Summer morning fields.

Fragment

On my way to city court
to be judged again,
I pick up a small stone.

The month is March;
it will be Easter soon.
I put the stone in my pocket;
it is that I feel the need
for deliverance and maybe
if I do this.

My hands are sweaty;
my fervent vain wish
is that I had never
been in jail
that first time.

I put the stone in my other hand
and caress it with my fingertips.
I find it is moist
and realize it is a fragment
of the earth center
and I know that it is
my redemption.

Notes on the Steps of the San Diego Bus Depot

Across the street
America is putting together
another Federal Building.

The Wisconsin Horse
looks through the chainlink fence.
He turns and tells me with his eyes.

I discover Marge Piercy
in a poetry newspaper.
Her thick sensual lips
are about to move
upon the earth.
I wonder if her dark eyes
are always seeing
beyond the farthest ridge.
Her words slant into me and resonate
and will echo
for a long time.
For centuries maybe.

I don't think the sky will fall today,
but I need a few surprises badly.

East of San Diego

I tell the bus driver
but he doesn't hear,
"Keep to the hills
and avoid America
if you can.
I'm a fugitive
from bad, futureless dreams
in Southern California."

Crow

"Did you see any crows
in San Diego?"

One, once in the desert
southeast of San Diego,
watched as he slid
on his wind road
across the valley
toward El Centro,
probably stopped
that night
by the Salton Sea.
I wondered how
he made it look so easy.

Returned from California

At the park
yesterday afternoon,
I found a dead crow
by the roots of a cottonwood.

Death is a bundle
of black feathers,
leather-lined dry holes
for eyes,
withered yellow feet.

Other crows
hollered from branches
above a scatter
of human garbage.
They forget easy enough.

Right now, I'm too tired
to scheme things,
but that will return
soon enough.
Dreams gather quickly
like Spring crows,
and they scatter.

Pain

Sometimes there's the slow,
slow unnecessary hurt.
My poor body is being devoured;
it is disintegrating.
The twinge comes from under,
tears the sacred flesh given me,
leaves no seeds for regeneration.
I should have taken her advice.
"You know, you should stay here
a long time by this ocean
and just sit and listen."

Wind and Glacier Voices

Laguna man said,
I only heard that glacier scraping
once, thirty thousand years ago.
My daughter was born then.
                    —a storytelling, continuing
                        voice—

West of Yuma, a brown man murmurs
the motion of the solar wind.
                    —a harsh, searing
                        voice—

Please don't tell me
how to live;
I've always lived this way.
                    —a protesting
                        voice—

The last time I was in Fargo
I thought I heard the echo
of a glacier scraping.
                    —a remembering,
                        beckoning
                        voice—

And the wind, solar,
the big wind will come.
Solar, it will come.
It will pass by and through
and with everything.
                    —a longing, whispering,
                        prophetic
                        voice—

Albuquerque Back Again: 12/6/74

After leaving Joy at class,
Rainy falls asleep
on the way back to the house.
Her head droops,
and I pull parka hood carefully
around her head.
Small round face, the wind
catches black hair,
puppy hair.
She sleeps, this child—
never mind the traffic
and ordinary insanity
of people going places
they might not actually know
the destinations of.

Day with blue sky,
cloud fluffs.
        Look to see
the mountains, and they are there,
the late Autumn sun sketching
crags and shadows, knife edge
of stone and granite ridge.

Yesterday, turning south
for New Mexico at San Luis,
Coyote looked at the mountains
and said, "We'll see you again,"
and prayed for safety, strength,
and the ability to see beauty.
It was beginning to snow then.

East of Tucumcari

I asked to get off
sixteen miles east of Tucumcari,
and the busdriver asked,
"Where are you going?"
I was coming home.

I saw the brown water
falling from a rock.
It felt so good
to touch the green moss.
A woman between
the mountain ridges
of herself—
it is overwhelming.

I could even smell
the northern mountains
in the water.

Watching You

for Joy

I watch you
from the gentle slope
where it is warm
by your shoulder.
My eyes are closed.
I can feel the tap
of your blood
against my cheek.
Inside my mind,

I see the gentle move
ment of your valleys,
the undulations
of slow turnings.
Opening my eyes,
there is a soft dark
and beautiful butte
moving up and then down
as you breathe.
There are fine
and very tiny ferns
growing, and I can
make them move
by breathing.
I watch you with my skin
moving upon yours,
and I have known you well.

Bend in the River

Flicker flies by.
His ochre wing
is tied to prayer sticks.
Pray for mountains,
the cold strong shelter.

Sun helps me to see
where Arkansas River
ripples over pebbles.
Glacial stone moves slowly;
it will take a while.

A sandbank cuts sharply
down to a poplar log
buried in damp sand.

Shadow lengths tell me
it is afternoon.

There are tracks
at river's edge, raccoon,
coyote, deer, crow,
and now my own.

My sight follows
the river upstream
until it bends.
Beyond the bend
is more river
and, soon, the mountains.
We shall arrive,
to see, soon.

THE FOURTH: THE RAIN FALLS

Earth Woman

for Joy

This woman has been shaping
mountains
millions of years and still
her volcanoes erupt
with continuous mysteries.

How gentle
her movements, her hands,
soft wind,
warm rain,
the moving pain
of pleasure

we share.

Spreading Wings on Wind

*a plane ride from Rough
Rock to Phoenix Winter
Indian 1969*

I must remember
that I am only one part
among many parts,

not a singular eagle
or one mountain. I am
a transparent breathing.

Below are dark lines of stone,
fluff of trees, mountains
and the Earth's People—all of it,
the Feather in a prayer.

Faint, misty clouds,
a sudden turbulence,
and steady, the solid earth.

"It looks like a good road,"
from Piñon to Low Mountain.
It branches off to First Mesa
and then Second and Third Mesa.
The Hopi humanity
which is theirs and ours.

Three of the Navajo Mountains
in our vision, "Those mountains
over there, see their darkness
and strength, full of legends,
heroes, trees, the wind, Sun."

East, West, North, and South.
Those Directions and Mountains.
Mountain Taylor, San Francisco Peak,
Navajo Mountain, Dibentsaa.
The Navajo mind must have been
an eagle that time.

Breathe like this on the feather
and cornfood like this, this way.

Sometime before there were billboards
advertising Meteor Crater,
there must have been one hell of a jolt,
flame and then silence.
After many years, flowers and squirrels,
snow streaking down inside the cone.

Over Winslow is the question,
"Who the hell was Winslow, some cowboy?"
A miner? Surveyor? Missionary?
The forests are neatly trimmed hedges;
mines are feeble clawings at the earth.

What the hell are you doing to this land?
My grandfather hunted here, prayed,
dreamt; one day there was a big jolt,
flame, and then silence,
just the clouds forming.

For Nanao

*a Japanese friend poet who
visited Canyon de Chelly*

That time you came back
and told us
about meeting a Navajo woman
on the canyon's rim,
you were happy and smiling.

You said, "We were talking,
smiling and gesturing to each."

Yes, Nanao,
you must have been truly.

The two languages,
Navajo and Japanese,
origins from the monumental age
of glacial Asia,
it is all true.

You must have been
mother and son then,
or sister and brother,
or lover and lover.

I can see you smiling,
remembering that time
in millennia. I can see
the lights in your eyes.

The Boy and Coyote

*for a friend, Ed Theis, met
at VAH, Ft. Lyons
Colorado, November and
December 1974*

You can see the rippled sand rifts
shallow inches below the surface.
I walk on the alkalied sand.
Willows crowd the edges of sand banks
sloping to the Arkansas River.

I get lonesome for the young afternoons
of a boy growing at Acoma.
He listens to the river,
the slightest nuance of sound.

Breaking thin ice from a small still pool,
I find Coyote's footprints.
Coyote, he's always somewhere before you;
he knows you'll come along soon.
I smile at his tracks which are not fresh
except in memory and say a brief prayer
for good luck for him and for me and thanks.

All of a sudden, and not far away,
there are the reports of a shotgun,
muffled flat by saltcedar thickets.
Everything halts for several moments,
no sound; even the wind holds to itself.
The animal in me crouches, poised immobile,
eyes trained on the distance, waiting
for motion again. The sky is wide;
blue is depthless; and the animal
and I wait for breaks in the horizon.

Coyote's preference is for silence
broken only by the subtle wind,
uncanny bird sounds, saltcedar scraping,
and the desire to let that man free,
to listen for the motion of sound.

My Children, and a Prayer for Us

Raho says, "You take a feather
and this white stuff,
and you let it fall to the ground;
that's praising."

Yes, son, it is,
and your words will always
remain like that.
Be strong and think clear thoughts,
always see the wholeness
of what is around you,
touch their realness,
feel the vibrating motion
of mornings,
exult in your presence
with the humility

that true knowledge imparts,
that you are one part
among many and all parts.

Rainy
daughter dark eyes
touch wind quiver
the inwards of mountain power
full flow
know the innate tension
that is your life
in stones leaves insects
lights in frost crystals;
simple words I wish
for you
ours to share.

Allspirit, pray with me
my humble prayers: I give you
myself, my only hope I know,
knowing nothing else
except that I have truly nothing
to offer except that which
you have given to me;
I give it back to you.

Thank you.

Four Deetseyamah Poems

I wake this morning to snow,
snow everywhere
and a heavy dry mist
which begins to clear
around 8:30.
Outside is a bitter

windless bite
on ears and cheeks,
and the snow is powdery dry,
drifted where the wind
has blown it.
"It snowed on Saturday,"
my mother and father tell me
and describe their stay
last week at Aacqu
helping with the Winterprayers.
My mother says, "We got cold
the other night because
the door had opened
during the night.
I had felt cold
and I got up once
to put wood in the stove
and went back to bed.
Later, I was cold again
and getting up to build the fire
I saw light coming in
through the door.
It was already getting morning.
Looking over at your father
who was sleeping by the west wall,
I called to him,
but he didn't answer.
Checking his bed, I found him
all rolled up in his blankets,
and I told him that the door
must have opened and there was snow
drifted inside the house.
No wonder we were so cold,"
she says, and we all laugh.

It's good in the morning
to eat breakfast
with my mother and my father,
drink hot coffee,
see the morning life.

My nephews and my nieces
are going to school;
they run through the snow,
puffs of snow kicking off their shoes,
running for the school bus.
On this cold morning,
Louise's husband starts cars,
first Louise's, then Myrna's,
and then Aunt Katie's.
After a while, they all leave.
The sky is very clear winter blue.

Looking north and seeing
Kaweshtima, the strong mountain
is a prayer.
On cold winter days, the mountain
seems taller and bigger,
the distinctions made by the contrast
of light and dark, the differences
made sharper and clearer,
the clarity of space.
It occurs to me again
that wherever I have been,
I have never seen a Mountain
that has stood so clearly
in my mind; when I have needed
to envision my home, when loneliness
for myself has overcome me,
the Mountain has occurred.
Now, I see it sharing its being
with me, praying.

On Friday, Joy and I talked
about sense of presence.
What is it? How does it come about?
I think it has to do
with a sense of worth, dignity,
and how you fit with occasion, place,
people, and time.
It's also a physical thing,
carriage of body,

hand and head movements,
eyes fixed upon specific points.
And then it is an ability
which is instinctive and spiritual
to convey what you see
to those around you.
Essentially, it is how you fit
into that space which is yourself,
how well and appropriately.

My Mother and My Sisters

My oldest sister wears thick glasses
because she can't see very well.
She makes beautifully formed pottery.
That's the thing about making dhyuuni;
it has to do more with a sense of touching
than with seeing because fingers
have to know the texture of clay
and how the pottery is formed from lines
of shale strata and earth movements.
The pottery she makes is thinwalled
and has a fragile but definite balance.
In other words, her pottery has a true ring
when it is tapped with a finger knuckle.

Here, you try it;
you'll know what I mean.

The design that my mother is painting
onto the bowl is done with a yucca stem brush.
My other sister says, "Our mother,
she can always tell when someone else has used
a brush that she is working with," because
she has chewed it and made it into her own way.

She paints with movements whose origin
has only to do with years of knowing
just the right consistency of paint,
the tensile vibrancy of the yucca stem,
and the design that things are supposed to have.

She can always tell.

My mother talks about one time.
"One time, my sister and I
and this one lady—she was
a fat woman—went to roast piñons.
Stuwahmeeskuunaati, over that way."
To the east of Aacqu the mesa cliffs
are red, brown, and white sandstone;
there are piñon trees there.
"We left in the morning
and walked up to the first level,
not on top, where there was a lot
of piñons that year.
We had to get the piñons
in their cones from the trees
and dig a hole and bury them
and then build a fire on top.
It took quite a while
to do that, like it does.
And then we got them out
and let them cool,
and then we gathered them
up and put them on our backs
in sacks. We started back
to Aacqu." It's a long ways
across the valley, sandhills,
grasses, brush, cottonwoods,
gullies, cacti. "When we got
to this one place, the woman said,
'This is where Maashadruwee lives.
You have to holler.'
You're supposed to yell or holler.
We prayed with cornmeal

and the lady said, 'Please,
Maashadruwee, make Aacqu closer
to us.' And we started again,
but before we got to Aacqu
onto the south trail,
it grew dark.
We knew that our relatives
would worry about us.
And sure enough, the woman's husband
was looking and he met us
at the bottom of the trail.
When we got to south of the church,
my father met us—he had come
to look for us too."
My mother chuckles with the memory
of it, when she was a young girl.
"I don't know if my sister
remembers, but I do, very clearly.
But I don't know
what my age was then."

What Joy Said on Two Occasions

One of our neighbors is a young man
with one leg thinner and shorter
than the other, and a couple of weeks ago
I saw him pouring charcoal fluid
on an anthill several yards from his door,
and then he set fire to it.
Walking over to him I said,
"Why you doing that for, man?"

Charcoal fluid and burning ants smell ugly.
I told Joy about it.

A couple of days ago
that guy was limping toward his door,
and I said that he must have the limp
because he had polio as a child.

Joy said, "It's probably because
he burns ants."
It's probably because she's Creek
that makes her know that.

This morning, while I was waking up,
she said, "I got up and went back to bed
two times. When I get up now,
it's almost still dark."

Later, when I got up and it was quiet,
I looked out that window that I busted
one night when I was drunk,
and outside was so clear and good
that I felt lonely for all those things
I haven't done lately.

Juanita, Wife of Manuelito

after seeing a photograph
of her in Dine Baa-Hani

I can see by your eyes
the gray in them like by Sonsela Butte,
the long ache
that comes about when I think
about where the road climbs
up onto the Roof Butte.

I can see
the whole sky
when it is ready to rain

over Whiskey Creek,
and a small girl
driving her sheep
and she looks so pretty
her hair tied up
with a length of yarn.

I can see
by the way you stare
out of a photograph
that you are a stern woman
informed by the history
of a long walk
and how it must have felt
to leave the canyons
and the mountains of your own land.

I can see, Navajo woman,
that it is possible for dreams
to occur, the prayers full of the mystery
of children, laughter, the dances,
my own humanity, so it can last unto forever.

That is what I want to teach my son.

A Pretty Woman

We came to the edge
of the mesa
and looked below.

We could see
the shallow wash
snaking down
from the cut
between two mesas,
all the way from Black Mountain;

and the cottonwoods
from that distance
looked like a string of turquoise,

and the land was a pretty woman
smiling at us
looking at her.

Bony

My father brought that dog home
in a gunny sack.

The reason we called it Bony
was because it was skin and bones.

It was a congenital problem
or something that went way back
in its dog's history.

We loved it without question,
its history and ours.

Two Acoma Pictures

LITTLE WREN I NEED A SONG

Little Wren, this morning, quickly
make me a song
made of sandstone clefts,
a bit of yucca growing there.

Quickly, my friend, just a bit
of song which goes:
    cool morning shadow
    sandstone ledge mica glints
    sun will rise from Chuska horizon.

TWO WOMEN AT THE NORTHERN CISTERN

Tadpole says,
    Where were you last night.
    I was waiting for you all night.
    I know you think I am still young.
    But I am getting bigger; watch.

    Here, drink from my well.

For Rainy's Book

Poetry is
the silence
of Sun and Quuti.

A Deer Dinner

After you have gotten a deer,
a dinner is given for it.
Kudra quuya comes to the dinner,
and she acts like a silly old gal.
She teases with you
like you were her man, making promises.
And then she takes the eyes
out of the deer's head
which is boiling in a big pot.
And then she blesses you with prayer
for your virility and good luck
and not to disappoint her promises.

A Snowy Mountain Song

I like her like that,

a white scarf
tied to her head,
the lines on her face
are strong.

Look, the snowy mountain.

Yuusthiwa

"Whenever people are driving along and stop
to offer Yuusthiwa a ride, he refuses
and says, 'I still have my legs,' "
my father says, saying it like the old man,
a slow careful drawl. And my mother corrects him,
" 'While I'm still able to walk.' "
Yuusthiwa has been sick lately;
either something fell on him
or else he got bit by something, she heard.
Apparently, he still gets around though
pretty much because like my father says
one fellow had said, " 'That old man,
he's still tom-catting around, visiting.'
You see him in Acomita along the road
or in McCartys." I chuckle at the expression
picturing the old guy in mind; after all,
Yuusthiwa is only 114 years old at last count.

"One time, David and I were coming
from Acomita," my father says, "and we stopped
for him. Recognizing me, he got in and said
'Ahku Tsai-rrhlai kudha.' And as we drove
westwards up this way, he told us things.
I had asked him, 'Naishtiya, how do you come
to live as many years as you have, to be so fortunate
as to mature as healthy and firm as you are?'
And he said, 'If you live enjoying and appreciating
your life, taking care of yourself, caring for
and being friendly with others; if you use the plants
that grow around here, seeing and knowing
that they are of use, boiling them into medicine
to use in the right way in caring for yourself,
cleansing and helping your body with them;
that's the way I have lived.' That's the way
he said it," my father says.

Hawk

Hawk
sweeps
clear through
the background
which is sky
and mountain ledge.
—Old Chuska Mountain,
my friend, shelter—
His immense knowledge
of wind,
his perception
of circling slow wind,
his edge of wing
on air trail

straightens then suddenly
overhead,
directly above us,
the pines.

This man, he knows
what he is doing.

Buzzard

Climbing suddenly
out of a ravine,
we saw a black buzzard
working at carrion.
The air was rancid,
not much wind,

and the dust was hot
and still, like the day.

Quietly now, pull
the breath back
into the body.

Sky is very endless
and dry; no clouds.

The buzzard doesn't see
us as it pokes
upon the animal wreckage,
rags of skin and entrails,
poor bones, claws.

Suddenly, the wind shifts,
air changes, and dust
sweeps to the bird,
and it looks toward us,
suddenly fearful, the briefest
recognition in its eyes,

and then with a great clatter
of wings, it rushes
away, a torn entrail sodden
with rot falls behind it
into the dust.

Breath is let out,
and the hot wind reeks again.

I've heard an older man say, "They take the eyes first." I wonder why?
I think it must have to do with ritual, some distinct memory consis-
tent with the history of its preceding generations. And the buzzard
pays ritual homage to the memory of its line, the tradition that insures
that things will continue. Yes, that must be what it is. Eyes have a qual-
ity of regenerating visions which must continue first and last of all.

Dry Root in a Wash

The sand is fine grit
and warm to the touch.
An old juniper root
lies by the cutbank of sand;
it lingers, waiting
for the next month of rain.

I feel like saying,
It will rain, but you know
better than I these centuries
don't mean much
for anyone to be waiting.

Upstream, toward the mountains,
the Shiwana work for rain.

They know we're waiting.

Underneath the fine sand
it is cool
with crystalline moisture,
the forming rain.

Curly Mustache, 101-Year-Old Navajo Man

Thin, strong man.
Wears glasses
with stretch band
knotted behind head.

White mustache
hangs long
sides of mouth.

How long this cricket
been around?

Gray hat hangs
from chair armrest
at his side.

Motions
with long hand,
brown fingers
shape the mountain
ridge
of his knuckles.
Meadow wind
flows in channels
of his skin.

How many times
the mountain tops?
How many times
the roots?

Wears Penney's neoprene
soled ankle-high boots.

Voice is wind
down canyon—
tiny headwater wind
from beneath granite
onto flat plain—
soothing cool wind.

A thousands of years
old cicada
here one moment,
one place
in millennia.

Tell me about glaciers.
Tell me if this is correct
what I have heard: the scrape
of a glacier sounds
like a touching wind
on stone, wood,
in someplace mountain dream.
I heard it from a Laguna man.
"A returning noise," he said,
"I got the story
from someone way back."

Old man, he points
with the old root,
the compass
of his hand knows
the waterholes,
watercourses,
the life flow
on earth places
of his mind.

Four Rains

for my daughter,
Rainy Dawn

FIRST RAIN

She looks at me
so brighteyed I can
see
so far
the mountains shining

when light slants
through rain
into roots
so delicate
they will probably last
always last.

SECOND RAIN

Voice
begins this way,
pointing things out.
I know that you will
listen for sounds
only you will
understand
the way they mean
to me.

THIRD RAIN

Brighteyed flash,
the tiniest mirrored
dreams reaching back
into granite who know
magic and mysteries;
there they are.
There.

FOURTH RAIN

Don't misunderstand me,
Shiwana.
She's my daughter.
I know what she's saying.
I know her name;
I know.

Morning Star

The space before dawn
holds morning star
in its true eye,
the center of all places
looking out
and always in,

the mountain shale
of still deep night
is all light
yet undiscovered,
solid and single,
a glacier without motion
until the gleam
of eternal orbits
shall be complete
and be alive,

for the morning star
finds that dawn
on its journey
through our single being,
the all that has depth
and completeness,
the single eye
through which we see
and are seen.

A Story of How a Wall Stands

At Aacqu, there is a wall
almost 400 years old
which supports hundreds
of tons of dirt and bones—
it's a graveyard built on a
steep incline—and it looks
like it's about to fall down
the incline but will not for
a long time.

My father, who works with stone,
says, "That's just the part you see,
the stones which seem to be
just packed in on the outside,"
and with his hands puts the stone and mud
in place. "Underneath what looks like loose stone,
there is stone woven together."
He ties one hand over the other,
fitting like the bones of his hands
and fingers. "That's what is
holding it together."

"It is built that carefully,"
he says, "the mud mixed
to a certain texture," patiently
"with the fingers," worked
in the palm of his hand. "So that
placed between the stones, they hold
together for a long, long time."

He tells me those things,
the story of them worked
with his fingers, in the palm
of his hands, working the stone
and the mud until they become
the wall that stands a long, long time.

For Joy to Leave Upon

December 28, 1974

Last night a bit before six,
walking from the river,
I saw my shadow by the moonlight.
Broken by the slight rise of a small hill,
ankle-high plants, earth imprints.
Had walked down to the old pear tree,
winter barren, stepped over loosened wire fence.

(Remembered one Autumn early evening
when I killed a flicker for feathers.
Wounded the bird with an airgun,
broke its wing. Flopping running bird
through underbrush, and when I caught it
I had to press its tight neck with my finger
and thumb. The warm struggle of muscle,
feathers, blood upon my skin, its gray eye,
the intense moments of a boy twelve years old.)

Fell once on snow and damp earth,
muscle pulled, sore for a while only though
and now can't tell which shoulder it was
I fell upon, the memory of pain gone.

The reflection of the silver moon
was broken on the river; it was a whipping flag.

The year I got out of the Army,
I tried to see if my grandfather's grapevines
would ever grow again.
I cut the dead vines down to the quick
of the main stem, inches above cluster of roots
(piled dry gray vines and burned them—
smoke is sweet and acrid) and pulled dirt
in circles around the roots and watered them.
But I left that Summer. Later,

I came back and saw a few green new shoots,
and then I left again.

Tonight, there is a waning moon.

It Doesn't End, Of Course

for Adelle, Spring 1970

It doesn't end.

In all growing
from all earths
to all skies,

in all touching
all things,

in all soothing
the aches of all years,

it doesn't end.

A Good Journey

PREFACE

There is a certain power that is compelling in the narrative of a story-
teller simply because the spoken word is so immediate and intimate.
It was the desire to translate that power into printed words that led me
to write *A Good Journey*. I wanted to show that the narrative style and
technique of oral tradition could be expressed as written narrative and
that it would have the same participatory force and validity as words
spoken and listened to. At the same time I wanted to have the poetry
show the energy that language is, the way that the energy is used and
transformed into vision, and the way this vision becomes knowledge
which engenders and affirms the substance and motion of one's life.

This book tries to achieve the direct impact that spoken narrative has.
If it does not succeed as words on a page, I think that it has considerable
effect when it is read aloud. For me, poetry and most prose stories should
be read aloud because the voice and other movements of the general body
language are critical to what is shared by speaker and listener. With-
out this sharing in the intellectual, emotional, physical, and spiritual
activity, nothing much happens. The poetic effect becomes muted,
sometimes dissipating totally. With *A Good Journey* I try to show
that the listener-reader has as much responsibility and commitment to
poetic effect as the poet. When this effect is achieved, the compelling
poetic power of language is set in motion toward vision and knowledge.

From an interview:

Why do you write? Who do you write for?

Because Indians always tell a story. The only way to continue is to tell a story and that's what Coyote says. The only way to continue is to tell a story and there is no other way. Your children will not survive unless you tell something about them—how they were born, how they came to this certain place, how they continued.

Who do you write for besides yourself?

For my children, for my wife, for my mother and my father and my grandparents and then reverse order that way so that I may have a good journey on my way back home.

TELLING

Telling About Coyote

Old Coyote . . .
"If he hadn't looked back
everything would have been okay
. . . like he wasn't supposed to,
                  but he did,
and as soon as he did, he lost all his power,
his strength."

". . . you know, Coyote
is in the origin and all the way
through . . . he's the cause
of the trouble, the hard times
that things have . . ."

"Yet, he came so close
to having it easy.
                  But he said,
"Things are just too easy . . ."
Of course he was mainly bragging,
shooting his mouth.
The existential Man,
Dostoevsky Coyote.

"He was on his way to Zuni
to get married on that Saturday,
and on the way there
he ran across a gambling party.

A number of other animals were there.
          He sat in
for a while, you know, pretty sure
of himself, you know like he is,
sure that he would win something.

                    But he lost
everything. Everything.
And that included his skin, his fur
which was the subject of envy
of all the other animals around.

Coyote had the prettiest,
the glossiest, the softest fur
that ever was. And he lost that.

          So some mice
finding him shivering in the cold
beside a rock felt sorry for him.
'This poor thing, beloved,'
they said, and they got together
just some old scraps of fur
and glued them on Coyote with piñon pitch.

And he's had that motley fur ever since.
You know, the one that looks like
scraps of an old coat, that one."

Coyote, old man, wanderer,
where you going, man?
Look up and see the sun.
Scorned, an old raggy blanket
at the back of the closet nobody wants.

"At this one conference
of all the animals there was a bird
with the purest white feathers.
His feathers were like, ah . . .
like the sun was shining on it
all the time but you could look at it
and you wouldn't be hurt by the glare.
It was easy and gentle to look at.
And he was Crow.

He was sitting at one side of the fire.
And the fire was being fed large pine logs,
and Crow was sitting downwind
from the fire, and the wind was blowing
that way . . .

        And Coyote was there.
He was envious of Crow because
all the other animals were saying,
'Wowee, look at that Crow, man,
just look at him,' admiring Crow.
Coyote began to scheme.
He kept on throwing pine logs into the fire,
ones with lots of pitch in them.
And the wind kept blowing,
all night long . . .
        Let's see,
the conference was about deciding
the seasons—when they should take place—
and it took a long time to decide that . . .
And when it was over, Crow was covered
entirely with soot. The blackest soot
from the pine logs.
And he's been like that since then."

"Oh yes, that was the conference
when Winter was decided
that it should take place
when Dog's hair got long.
        Dog said,
'I think Winter should take place
when my hair gets long.'
And it was agreed that it would. I guess
no one else offered a better reason."

        Who?
        Coyote?
O,
O yes, last time . . .
when was it,
I saw him somewhere

between Muskogee and Tulsa,
heading for Tulsy Town I guess,
just trucking along.

He was heading into some oakbrush thicket,
just over the hill was a creek.
Probably get to Tulsa in a couple days,
drink a little wine,
tease with the Pawnee babes,
sleep beside the Arkansas River,
listen to the river move,
. . . hope it don't rain,
hope the river don't rise.
He'll be back. Don't worry.
He'll be back.

They Come Around, The Wolves— And Coyote and Crow, Too

I told you about those Wolves.
You must talk with them,
meeting them someplace,
mountain trail, desert,
at your campfire,
and call them Uncle or Brother
but never Cousin or In-law.

"I am happy that you recognized us
and called us by the proper term,"
the Uncle said.
He was sitting there
with his hands held together,
met my eyes and then, being humble,
dropped his gaze to his hands.

"We come around
but we have a bad reputation,"
the Uncle said.
"I'm glad you came," I said.
He smiled but his eyes were sad.

"I was so pretty
and everyone liked me.
My voice especially.
Everyone would stop to listen,"
said Crow.

Coyote was silent.

"I would sing and sing.
Mocking Bird and even Parrot
were jealous of me.
My feathers would shine and shine,"
said Crow.

Coyote was silent.

Thinking Coyote wasn't listening,
Crow asked, "Are you sleeping?"

"No," Coyote said.

"Did you hear what I just said?"
asked Crow.

"Yes," said Coyote.

And Crow waited for Coyote's comment.
When it didn't come, he decided to sing.

"Cawr, cawr, cawr," Crow sang.

"Stop," said Coyote.

Crow waited for the favorable comment.
He closed his eyes and made ready to bow.

Coyote silently crept away.

"Are you my friend?" asked Coyote.
"One can't be too choosey," said Crow.

Hesperus Camp, July 13, Indian 1971

Marge and Susan came up last night.
"Hello."
Faces beyond the edge of dim firelight.
"Hi. Who's that?"
"Me."
"Simon, how are you?"
"Okay."

Went to get more wood.
Fire glowed up again.
Was going to go to bed,
but I was glad they came.

Susan is from Massachusetts.
"What do you think about the Southwest?"
"Well," she said, "I wouldn't
want to live here."

You really can't tell anyone
about beauty.
They just have to see for themselves.

We made small talk.

"Buster left town, cops gave him
twenty-four hours to get out.
Told that Indian to go back
to the reservation."

"Flower was up, says he's working."
"Unbelievable."

"I don't really know much myself."
"Nobody does, I guess."

"You go to school, Susan?"
"No. Haven't been to school
for a long time."
"Good girl."

"You got a cigarette?"
"Yeah, sure."
Lit up, pulled smoke in deeply.
"Thanks."
And etcetera small talk,
piñon wood coals crackling.

They were on the way to Monument Valley.
"If you can, climb up on Black Mountain,"
I told them, "and look north. Wow!
you'll see all of Monument Valley,

> *I can see it, the red and brown monoliths*
> *reaching for God, the ocean dried up*
> *just a couple million years ago,*
> *the fish are still squiggling in solid rock,*
> *the footprints of gods are still fresh.*

or you can look south from the Utah side.
It might rain, and it will look all fresh and new.

> *Crawling out of primordial swamp*
> *the gods' children, look, look—*
> *they are coming.*

"If you can, drive by Canyon de Chelly.
You ever been there? Take a long look
at the Lukachukai cliff face at evening,
the purple and the blue changing,
the evening of a day before another new day."

> *I get lonesome talking and thinking about it,*
> *and I stop.*

After a while, Susan and Marge say goodnight.
"We've got to get up early to leave."

"Goodnight."

The last of the firelight dimmed away
and the Milky Starway swept so quietly by
and so far away.

Brothers and Friends

Laugh at Magpie this morning.
He was telling stories
all morning at the top
of his lungs, sitting on a nearby pine.

Magpie, you clown. Longtail,
you surely act goofy.
Get a job, be a good American.
Hey, it's good to laugh with you,
to enjoy the life.

Had a visit from Skunk last night.
He went and ate my last bit of butter
and put trash into some juice.
And then he must have gotten
into the tuna casserole
I was saving for lunch.
Ah well, hope he didn't get sick.

Owl, a lone, hollow wood sound.
The night, windborne,
echoed upon itself.
Several nights ago was
the first time I heard it again.
I got frightened, worried.
And last night, Owl again,
but at peace now, the sound
was a welcome meaning.
I thought about the wind, echoes,
earth, origin, prayer wings.

Magpie.
Skunk.
Owl.
All are my brothers and friends.

A San Diego Poem: January–February 1973

THE JOURNEY BEGINS

My son tells his aunt,
"You take a feather,
and you have white stuff in your hand,
and you go outside,
and you let the white stuff fall to the ground
That's praising."

In the morning, take cornfood outside,
say words within and without.
Being careful, breathe in and out,
praying for sustenance, for strength,
and to continue safely and humbly,
you pray.

SHUDDERING

The plane lifts off the ground.
The shudder of breaking from earth
gives me a split second of emptiness.
From the air, I can only give substance
and form to places I am familiar with.
I only see shadows and darkness
of mountains and the colored earth.

The jet engines drone heavily.
Stewardesses move along the aisles.
Passengers' faces are normally bland,
and oftentimes I have yearned, achingly,
for a sharp, distinctive face, someone
who has a stark history, even a killer
or a tortured saint, but most times
there is only the blandness.

I seek association with the earth.
I feel trapped, fearful of enclosures.
I wait for the Fasten Seat Belt sign
to go off, but when it does
I don't unfasten my belt.

The earth is red in eastern Arizona,
mesa cliffs; the Chinle formation
is an ancient undersea ridge lasting
for millions of years.
I find the shape of whale still lingers.
I see it flick gracefully by Sonsela Butte
heading for the Grand Canyon.

I recite the cardinal points of my Acoma life,
the mountains, the radiance coming
from those sacred points, gathering
into the center.
I wonder: what is the movement
of this journey in this jet above the earth?

Coming into L.A. International Airport,
I look below at the countless houses,
row after row, veiled by tinted smog.
I feel the beginnings of apprehension.
Where am I? I recall the institutional prayers
of my Catholic youth but don't dare recite them.
The prayers of my native selfhood
have been strangled in my throat.

The Fasten Seat Belt sign has come back on
and the jet drone is more apparent in my ears.
I picture the moments in my life
when I have been close enough to danger
to feel the vacuum prior to death
when everything stalls.
The shudder of returning to earth
is much like breaking away from it.

UNDER L.A. INTERNATIONAL AIRPORT

Numbed by the anesthesia of jet flight,
I stumble into the innards of L.A. International.
Knowing that they could not comprehend,
I dare not ask questions of anyone.
I sneak furtive glances at TV schedule consoles
and feel their complete ignorance of my presence.
I allow an escalator to carry me downward;
it deposits me before a choice of tunnels.
Even with a clear head, I've never been good
at finding my way out of American labyrinths.
They all look alike to me. I search
for a distinct place, a familiar plateau,
but in the tunnel, on the narrow alley's wall,
I can only find bleak small-lettered signs.
At the end of that tunnel, I turn a corner
into another and get the unwanted feeling
that I am lost. My apprehension is unjustified
because I know where I am I think.
I am under L.A. International Airport,
on the West Coast, someplace called America.
I am somewhat educated, I can read and use a compass;
yet the knowledge of where I am is useless.
Instead, it is a sad, disheartening burden.
I am a poor, tired wretch in this maze.
With its tunnels, its jet drones, its bland faces,
TV consoles, and its emotionless answers,
America has obliterated my sense of comprehension.
Without this comprehension, I am emptied
of any substance. America has finally caught me.
I meld into the walls of that tunnel
and become the silent burial. There are no echoes.

SURVIVAL THIS WAY

Survival, I know how this way.
This way, I know.
It rains.

Mountains and canyons and plants
grow.
We traveled this way,
gauged our distance by stories
and loved our children.
We taught them
to love their births.
We told ourselves over and over
again,
"We shall survive this way."

Like myself, the source of these narratives is my home. Sometimes my father tells them, sometimes my mother, sometimes even the storyteller himself tells them.

*"I don't know how it started,
but this is the story:*

                    One time,
the Kawaikamehtitra—the Laguna people—
were having a rabbit hunt.
Tchaiyawahni ih—as they say in Laguna.
But in Acoma, it means
'hunting and killing each other.'
Among them was an Acoma
who was an in-law to the Lagunas.

At the beginning of the hunt,
the Field Chief gives instructions and bids
the people to pay heed to the rules
and to be careful not to harm each other.
He called to the people,
'Now, you can go out and hunt,
but you must be especially careful
that you don't kill Coyote because

some of you are clan relatives of his.'
There were some Coyote clan people in the hunt.
And he repeated,
'You can kill anything but don't kill Coyote.'

And so the Lagunas and the one Acoma
set out to hunt.
They went out like they do,
encircling the rabbits,
finding and killing them until at one point,
suddenly, Coyote was rousted out
from under a rock ledge
and he ran in the direction of the Acoma.
And the Acoma killed him.

One of the Coyote clan relatives saw it,
and he called, 'Coyote People, Coyote People,
our relative has been killed.
Come here, come here, our poor beloved relative
has been killed by this Acoma.'
And the Coyote People came and they mourned
their relative who was laid out at their feet.
They looked at the Acoma, and they cried angrily,
'Sthuudzhishu Aacqumeh eh, ahrhehmah,' meaning
'You confounded no-good dirty Acoma.'
And they began to chase him toward Acoma.
But as the Coyote People were chasing
and hollering at the Acoma,
Coyote suddenly jumped up and ran away.
The Coyote People stopped chasing and cussing
the Acoma and said that he could come back
and be an in-law to the Lagunas again.

I don't know if the story is true or not,
but that's the story I heard,"
my father said.

Sometimes Coyote is Pehrru.
Sometimes Pehrru is Coyote.
Sometimes they're one and the same.

This one is about Pehrru's wonderful kettle.

One day,
Pehrru was cooking at his camp.
He had a kettle of meat and corn
which he had just taken out of the ashes and coals.
The food had been buried, cooking all day long.
And he put the meat and corn on top
of the ashes and coals.
Just then,
a troop of sandahlrrutitra—soldiers—
came along.
They saw Pehrru busy at cooking,
and they saw the kettle,
and they smelled the good food.
The kettle was really boiling away,
they could see that, but they didn't see any fire.

"Guwahdze, Pehrru," the soldiers said in greeting.
"Dahwah eh," Pehrru said. He kept on being busy.

"You are sure busy with your cooking,"
the soldiers said.
"Hah uh," Pehrru said.

The soldiers were very curious
about the boiling kettle of stew.
They marvelled at how it was boiling
and there was no fire they could see.

"Your stew is boiling so beautifully,"
the soldiers said.
"Hah uh, it is boiling," Pehrru agreed, casually.

Finally,
curiosity getting the best of them,
the soldiers asked,
"How is it that the stew is boiling
when there is no fire under your kettle?"
Noting their overly eager curiosity,
Pehrru said, "Oh, it's just that that's the kind
of kettle it is. It boils like that by itself."

"That must be a wonderful kettle,"

the soldiers marvelled.
"Hah uh, it is," Pehrru said, nonchalantly,
"it is quite useful."

The soldiers talked among themselves
and then, without wanting to appear too eager,
they said to Pehrru, "Compadre, do you think
you can give us that wonderful kettle?"
Pehrru kept on being busy at cooking
and then he turned to them and said,
"Tsah dzee wah guwah nehwadi shrouwah drumanoh."

The kettle was really boiling away.
The smell of the meat and corn was delicious.
Indeed it was an amazing, wonderful kettle.
They had to have it, and the soldiers said,
"Well, let us buy the kettle from you."

Pehrru said,
"I don't think I can sell it to you;
it's such a favorite of mine," but he saw
that the soldiers were ready to bargain treasures
for the kettle. He pretended to be less reluctant
to part with his kettle.

They bargained.
The soldiers making an offer
and Pehrru holding back,
the soldiers raising their price
and Pehrru seeming to hold back less and less.
Until the soldiers said,
"We will give you your weight in gold
for the kettle."

And Pehrru, pretending a sorrowful reluctance, said,
"You have made me such a generous offer
for my beloved wonderful kettle, but I think
it is a fair price. Henah, you have bought it."

And the sandahlrrutitra brought Pehrru
his weight in gold and Pehrru gave them
the plain old smoke-blackened kettle
and they rode away . . .

And another one:

One time,
four people were eating together.
They saw Pehrru approaching them.
He was coming up the road.

One of them said,
"There comes Pehrru.
Don't anyone invite him to sit down and eat.
He's much of a liar."
The four kept on eating.

Pehrru got to where they were,
and he said, "Guwahdze."
They answered, "Dahwah eh,"
and they kept on eating.
Nobody invited Pehrru to sit down and eat.

"Wah trou yatawah?" Pehrru asked.
And they answered, "Hah uh, wahstou yatawah."
("Are you eating?"
"Yes, we're eating.")
Pehrru stood around watching them eat.

To make conversation,
one of the four asked,
"Where are you coming from?"
And Pehrru said,
"Oh, I'm coming from nowhere special."

After a bit more silence, another asked,
"Dze shru tu ni, Pehrru?"
And Pehrru answered,
"Oh, as usual I don't know much of anything."
The four kept on eating
and Pehrru kept standing, watching them eat.
And then he said,
"Oh wait, I do know a bit of something,"
and he paused until he was sure

they were waiting for him to go on,
and then he said,
"When I was coming here, I saw some cows."

Pretending to show little interest,
one said, "Oh well, one usually sees
some cows around."

And Pehrru said, "Yes, yes, that's true.
Well, one of them had just given birth
to some calves."

And one of them said,
"Oh well, you know, usually cows
give birth to calves."

"The cow was feeding her calves,"
Pehrru said.

"Oh well, that's what cows usually do,
feed their calves," one of the four said.

And then Pehrru said,
"The cow had given birth to five calves.
One of them, beloved, was just standing around,
looking hungry, not feeding because
as you know, cows usually only have four nipples."

And the four, realizing the meaning
of Pehrru's story, looked at each other
and said,
"Shtsu dzeshu, Pehrru. Sit down and eat."
Smiling, Pehrru joined them in eating.

When it was time to get a meal,
Pehrru was known to be a shrewd man.

How to make a good chili stew— this one on July 16, a Saturday, Indian 1971

for all my friends who like it

It's better to do it outside
or at sheepcamp
or during a two or three day campout.
In this case, we'll settle
for Hesperus, Colorado
and a Coleman stove.

INGREDIENTS

Chili	(Red, frozen, powdered, or dry pods. In this case, just powdered because that's all I have.)
Beef	(In this case, beef which someone who works in a restaurant in Durango brought this morning, leftovers, trim fat off and give some to the dog because he's a good guy. His name is Rex.)
Beef bullion	(Five or six cubes, maybe, for taste.)
Garlic	(About two large cloves. Smell it to know it's good.)
Salt and pepper	(You just have to test how much.)
Onion	(In this case, I don't have any, but if you do have some around, include it with much blessings.)
Hominy	(Preferably the homemade kind like we used to make at home. You soak kernels of corn in limewater overnight until the husks wash off easy. But storebought is okay too.)

DIRECTIONS

Put chile and some water into a saucepan with bullion, garlic which is
    diced, and salt and pepper and onion which I don't have and won't
    mention anymore because I miss it, and you shouldn't ever be
    anyplace without it, I don't care where.
And then put it on to barely boiling, cover and smell it once in a while
    with good thoughts in your mind, and don't worry too much about
    it except, of course, keep water in it so it doesn't burn, okay.
In the meantime, you can cut the meat (which, in this case, I should
    mention, was meant for Rex the dog but since it was left over from
    just last night and it's not bad—I know 'cause I tasted it—that's
    alright, but if you can afford it, cut the lean meat) into less than
    inch pieces and you don't have to measure, just cut it so it looks like
    cut meat.
Make sure you smell the chili in the saucepan once in a while and
    think of a song to go along with it. That's important.
More on meat, in the case it's not cooked leftovers from last night.
    Well, you put it into a pan with tiny diced garlic with a small pat of
    butter and meat fat and watch it turn brown and listen to it
    sizzle—a delightful sound—for as long as you want just so it doesn't
    burn and set aside and relax for a while.
Smelling and watching are important things, and you really shouldn't
    worry too much about it—I don't care what Julia Child says—but
    you should pay the utmost attention to everything, and that means
    the earth, clouds, sounds, the wind. All these go into the cooking.
And then you put everything into a pot—a cast iron one is best, like
    the one my Dad and I put a sheep's head into at sheepcamp with
    rice and pieces of bread dough for dumplings and buried it in the
    ashes and coals so it was cooked by the time we got back to camp in
    the evening from herding sheep.

FURTHER DIRECTIONS TO MAKE SURE IT'S GOOD

Don't forget about the chili.
Look all around you once in a while. (In this case, the La Plata
    Mountains in southern Colorado. It's going to rain soon on them
    and maybe here too if we're lucky.)

Don't let the Magpies get on your nerves. (Which is the case here
   because Edward and Susan Magpie's kids are here all by themselves.
   Ed and Su went someplace, maybe on vacation or to the big
   city—Relocation Welding School—and the kids are getting into all
   kinds of mischief. I throw them apples once in a while, but they're
   sassy and ornery, chattering and swearing and laughing all the time,
   acting big. If you see Ed and Su, please tell them everything's right
   on, their kids are getting big and you tell them to write. Maybe
   you'll see them around Oakland or Los Angeles, at the Indian
   Center.

If there are Magpies around, make sure you invite them, saying, "I
   want you all to come over for dinner. We've been wondering how
   you've all been. Your Aunts and Uncles and Grandfather will be
   there." Say it with great welcoming and sincerity and I'll betcha
   they'll come.

WAITING FOR IT TO GET DONE

Oh, maybe about two hours for the chili to simmer and then put in the
   hominy and cover with water and simmercook for another two
   hours.

   It's also good to have someone along,
   and in case they don't know how too good
   you can teach them, slowly and surely,
   until they're expert. It will take more than
   one time but that's okay and much better.
   It's best to do anytime.

AT LAST

Well, my friends, that's all there is to it,
   for the chili stew part, but as you well
   know there is more than that too. So good luck.
   And you can eat now.

And there is always one more story. My mother
was telling this one. It must be an old story but
this time she heard a woman telling it at one of
those Sunday meetings. The woman was telling
about her grandson who was telling the story
which was told to him by somebody else. All
these voices telling the story, including the voices
in the story—yes, it must be an old one.

One time,
(or like Rainy said, "You're sposed to say, 'Onesa ponsa
time,' Daddy")

there were some Quail Women grinding corn.
Tsuushki—Coyote Lady—was with them.
She was
grinding u-uuhshtyah—juniper berries.
I don't know why she wasn't grinding corn too—
that's just in the story.

It was a hot, hot day, very hot,
and the Quail Women got thirsty,
and they decided to go get some water to drink.
They said,
"Let's go for a drink of water,
and let's take along our beloved comadre."
So they said, "Comadre, let's all go
and get some water to drink."
"Shrow-uh,"
Coyote said.

The water was in a little cistern
at the top of a tall rock pinnacle
which stands southeast of Aacqu.
They walked
over there but they had to fly to get to the top.

The Quail Women looked at Tsuushki who couldn't fly
to the top because she had no feathers,
         and they felt
very sorry and sad for Tsuushki.

So they decided, "Let us give shracomadre
some of our feathers."
      The Quail Women said that
and they took some feathers out of themselves
and stuck them on Coyote.
        And then they all flew
to the top of the pinnacle where the water was.
They all drank their fill and Coyote
was the last to drink.
      While she was drinking
from the cistern, on her hands and knees,
the Quail Women decided to play a trick, a joke
on Coyote Lady.
     They said,
"Let's take the feathers from our comadre
and leave her here."
      "Alright," they all agreed,
and they did that, and they all left.

When Tsuushki had drank her fill of water
and was ready to descend the pinnacle,
she found that she could not
because she had no feathers to fly with anymore.
She felt very bad,
    and she sat down,
       wondering
what to do.
The rock pinnacle was too high up
to jump down from.

But, pretty soon,
    Kahmaasquu Dya-ow—
Spider Grandmother—came climbing over the edge
of the pinnacle to drink water also.

And Coyote thought to herself,
                              Aha,
I will ask my Grandmother to help me off.
She is always a wonderful helpful person.

So Coyote asked,
"Dya-ow Kahmaasquu, do you think you could help me
descend this pinnacle? You are always such
a wonderful helpful person."

And Spider Grandmother said,
                              "Why yes,
beloved one, I will help you.
Climb into my basket."
                              She pointed at a basket
tied at the end of her rope.
                              And then
she said, "But I must ask you one thing.
While I am letting you down,
you must not look up, not once,
not even just a little bit.
                              For if you do,
I will drop you.
And that is quite a long ways down."

"Oh, don't worry about that, Dya-ow,
I won't look up. I'm not that kind of person,"
Coyote promised.
                    "Alright then,"
Spider said, "Climb in
and I will let you down."

The basket began to descend,
                              down
                                    and
                                          down,
BUT on the way down,
                    Coyote looked up
(At this point, the voice telling the story
is that of the boy who said,

"But Tsuushki
looked up and saw her butt!")
and Spider Grandmother dropped the basket
and Coyote went crashing down.

Well, at this point, the story ends but,
as you know, it also goes on.
                              Well, sometime later,
the Shuuwimuu Guiguikuutchah—
Skeleton Fixer—came along.
He saw a scatter of bones at the foot of the pinnacle.
Skeleton Fixer said,
                    "Oh look,
some poor beloved one must have died.
I wonder who it may be?"
                         The bones
were drying white in the sun, lying around.
And Skeleton Fixer said,
                         "I think I will put
the bones together
and find out and he will live again."

And he joined the bones together,
                                    very carefully,
and when he had finished doing that,
he danced around them while he sang,

"Shuuwimuu shuuwimuu chuichukuu
Shuuwimuu shuuwimuu chuichukuu
Bah Bah."
          (which is to say)
Skeleton skeleton join together
Skeleton skeleton join together
Bah Bah.
          And the skeleton bones did,
and the skeleton jumped up,
and it was Coyote.

"Ah kumeh, Tsuushkitruda," Skeleton Fixer said.
Oh, it's just you Coyote—I thought
it was someone else.

And as Coyote ran away,
Skeleton Fixer called after her,

                              "Nahkeh-eh,
bah aihatih eyownih trudrai-nah!"
Go ahead and go, may you get crushed
by a falling rock somewhere!

NOTES FOR MY CHILD

Grand Canyon Christmas Eve 1969

(Later to lie down and sleep,
the earth—surrounded by trees—
for my bed.)

The fire is a higher blue
rhythm and melody.
The mist fills the carved earth.
Breathe: who did this?
River. That little river?
And time and wind and birds
and lizards, coyote, the whole earth
spirit of all those things.
Breathing the earth!

My son cries.
I hear him
in the forest.
He's snuggled down
like he was back
on Siberian ice,
the glacial winds howling.
O the stars
O the moon
O the earth
the trees the ground
We have come to pay respect
to you, my mother earth,

who makes all things
bless me
we are humble
bless my sons
make them strong
bless my wife
give her that subtle timelessness
of stones and mist and beauty
the strength
bless me who prays
awestruck.

Shake the log
and the fire flares up
into stars.
Watch the moon
for the earth's time
when it doesn't need time.
Moon sets in the crotch
of a piñon and the forest
is full of smoke.

Go to gather wood,
fall down once
on stones and damp sand,
arms are tired,
breathe heavily.
Peel and cut potatoes,
cut mutton arm
and put fat in the pan.
Put the mutton in,
give Raho some bread.
He wants meat.
Tell him gently to wait.
Get water for coffee,
rake out coals,
drink water which tastes
of mountain and roots,
put the pot
on coals to boil.
Wait.

Mutton sizzles in pan.
Pick out a coal
fallen into the meat.
Damn, the fire is hot,
pain on knuckles,
lick them with tongue.
Evening is getting colder.
Mutton smells good,
put in sliced potatoes,
sizzles, push coals
under the pan.
Wait.
Hunger mumbles in my belly.
And then everything is ready.
Toast bread on fork end.
But one more thing.
Feed the gods some bread,
meat, salt into the fire,
saying, Thank you, eat
with us.
And we eat, finally.

Mutton gets cold too fast.
Grease smoke from fat bits
I threw in the fire
smells good.
The pine wood fire
is a bit too hot
but it's good,
eating by the canyon,
the forest all around.

Nearby a U.S. Forest Service
sign reads:

KAIBAB NATIONAL FOREST
CAMP ONLY IN CAMPING AREAS
NO WOOD GATHERING
GO AROUND OTHER SIDE OF ENCLOSED AREA
&
DEPOSIT 85 CENTS FOR WOOD

This is ridiculous.
You gotta be kidding.
Dammit, my grandfathers
ran this place
with bears and wolves.
They even talked
with each others about it,
and you don't even listen.

And I got some firewood
anyway from the forest,
mumbling, Sue me.

The moon clock has moved
into the higher branches.
Stars cluster
in the pine tops.
I lie down on my earth bed.
Here it is possible
to believe legend,
heros praying on mountains,
making winter chants,
the child being born Coyote,
his name to be the Christ.
Here it is possible
to believe eternity.

My Children

Raho and I watched
a cabinet maker working
at wood.
His hands' movements
shifted wood
around easily, carefully,
knowing just the moment
to put wood to moving saw.
The smell of burnt,
hot wood and slight sweat.
"My son wanted to watch
you working at wood,"
I told the man.
The man looked up briefly,
nodded his head, his hands
stopping only a second.
Raho watching, watching.

Rainy and I watch
sparrows out the window.
They grub in damp earth,
looking for worms, beetles.
Rainy squeals.

"Like a little bird,"
one of my nieces said
on Easter Sunday.

One bird hops into a puddle,
ruffles its feathers,
pokes beak into the water
and shakes its head.
Rainy looks at me.
"A little bird," I tell her.

Speaking

I take him outside
under the trees,
have him stand on the ground.
We listen to the crickets,
cicadas, million years old sound.
Ants come by us.
I tell them,
"This is he, my son.
This boy is looking at you.
I am speaking for him."

The crickets, cicadas,
the ants, the millions of years
are watching us,
hearing us.
My son murmurs infant words,
speaking, small laughter
bubbles from him.
Tree leaves tremble.
They listen to this boy
speaking for me.

This Magical Thing

This, my son
moves his legs,
turns a circle
once
and then again,
a couple more times.

He stops,
looks at me
and laughs
for my approval
of this magical thing
he has done.

I laugh my happiness,
loving him,
loving the magic
of his movement,
of his laughter.
His eyes
look for my eyes,
find me
growing strong.

Notes For My Child

July 5, 1973, when she was born

Wake slow this morning.

Hear Joy moan,
stir around,
and get up sometime after five.

Bit of morning light.

Get up and wash,
put on two days-old coffee.

Later,
we walk for you
over to University Drug.

Sun slants
through trees,
cool morning.

See two cicadas.
One is dead,
the other is buzzing
trying to take off
from the sidewalk.

I want to turn back
and help it
to fly again,
but I realize
the inevitable.

Yesterday,
while chopping weeds,
I uncovered two chrysalis,
the cicadas within them
curled, soft yet.

We get to the hospital.
The taxi driver says, "Good luck."
"Okay, thanks." Smiling nervous.

Hospitals are consistent.
Crummy. We wait
for someone to notice us.

I tell Joy
to make herself visible.
She can't be anymore visible
she thinks than now,
her belly sticking out.

I ask where my wheelchair is
when Joy gets in hers
and is pushed down the hall
and into an elevator
by a fat unsmiling aide
who doesn't think
I am funny at all.

Upstairs and down a hall,
and Joy disappears
behind some doors.

I squat on the tile floor,
remember a poem Joy has written
about the story teller.

The aide walks by.
She smiles this time
and says, "Okay."
I say, "Okay," too.

Seven other people wait
and make small talk.
A couple of women
are rolled by.

I smile at the six women
and one guy.
A couple smile back.

When the women roll by
everything becomes somber
and slow.

. . . the Wisconsin Horse
is silent, looks through
the chainlink fence,
the construction going on
a mile away . . . .

Finally,
I get to join Joy.
She's getting anxious.
Can tell in her eyes,
movements, tremble
about her mouth.

A nurse tells me
to go to Admitting.
A girl asks me a question.
"Are you the responsible party?"
I say, "Yes."
She means money, of course.
Who's going to pay?
I mean I'm the father

of the child bringing life
and continuance.

I go back upstairs.
A woman on the other side
of the room moans a bit,
struggles in her sheets.
An older woman holds her hand.

Joy is pretty relaxed,
takes deep breaths
to make it easier.
Amazing how anyone can relax
at the eve of birth—
only a step along the way,
of course.
I ask Joy if it hurts,
realize it's a dumb
but important question.

A doctor comes along
and puts a plastic machine
upon Joy's belly
and flicks it on.
The doctor calls it
a doptone and says,
"Don't ask me why it's called that.
I don't know. It runs on batteries."

I call it
steady, gentle beating noises
called flesh, bones, blood,
runs on mysteries, dreams,
the coming child.

I am hungry now
but the hospital atmosphere
prevents any real hunger.
The repressiveness of institutions
has trained my stomach.
Tell myself to relax and say,
"When you come out, child,
let's go dance in a while, okay?"

Look out the window
and see the sun
and the parking lot.

Remember I wanted to write
something about that old dog,
kind of skinny and pathetic,
been hanging around our home
for a while, a week or so,
write a story or poem about it.

And then she was born.

. . . I will tell her
about the Wisconsin Horse . . . .

She was born then.

"She's as pretty as a silver dollar,"
said Ed Marlow, a miner
in Eastern Kentucky about Caroline Kennedy.
"She's just plain folks."

Albermarle County Sheriff says,
"We found nekkid women
with nekkid pubic hair offensive."

July 5, 1973 is now and soon enough

You come forth
the color of a stone cliff
at dawn,
changing colors,
blue to red,
to all the colors of the earth.

Grandmother Spider speaks
laughter and growing
and weaving things and threading them
together to make life to wear,
all these, all these.

You come out, child,
naked as that cliff at sunrise,
shorn of anything

except spots of your mother's blood.
You kept blinking your eyes
and trying to catch your breath.

In five more days,
they will come,
singing, dancing,
bringing gifts,
the stones with voices,
the plants with bells.
They will come.

Child, they will come.

Earth and Rain, The Plants & Sun

Once near San Ysidro
on the way to Colorado,
I stopped and looked.

The sound of a meadowlark
through smell of fresh cut alfalfa.

Raho would say,
"Look, Dad." A hawk

sweeping
   its wings

clear through
  the blue
of whole and pure
  the wind
    the sky.

It is writhing
overhead.
Hear. The Bringer.
      The Thunderer.

Sunlight falls
through cloud curtains,
a straight bright shaft.

It falls,
      it falls
  down
  to earth,
a green plant.

Today the Katzina come.
The dancing prayers.
Many times, the Katzina.
The dancing prayers.
It shall not end,
son, it will not end,
this love.

Again and again,
the earth is new again.
They come, listen, listen.
Hold on to your mother's hand.
They come.

O great joy, they come.
The plants with bells.
The stones with voices.
Listen, son, hold my hand.

Pout

Daughter
sits straddle-legged
on the floor. Smiles
as she turns the pages
of a catalogue. Toys,
books, clothes, rocky
horseys. Smiles and mur
murs. And then, watching
her, several pages stick
together, and the crinkle
of a frown edges on her fore
head and her lips purse
and push forward in con
cern. And I smile
and pout my mouth
in sympathy and love.

Burning River

I will tell my son over and over again,
"Do not let the rivers burn."
Mountains must stand
until winds and rains come,
and they—and only they—
will cause them to sink
back into the center
of that universal river
which is their's
and their children's,
Magpie, Bear, and Coyote too.

I will tell him over and over
and over again.

Joan, my hostess, was telling me about the river as she drove me from
Kent State to the airport. "This is the only river in America that ever
burned." The countryside is smalltown industrial America, settled
with small erecto-set plants for the making of small parts, things to
package things in, things to take things apart with. I am appalled and
try to smother the apprehension that makes me think that soon we
shall suffer many burning rivers.

We wait at the crossing.

The train shudders
with some evil disease.
The disease kills
even as it dies.
And the disease will be
at its furious work
until its frantic energy
will become its burning death.

And then the weakened spirit
will turn to the center
and become the cooled wind
and become the cooled rain
and wash the last vestige
of waste from our bones,
from our charred ligaments
and wash them back

to the River,
the River,
the River,
four times the River.

A Morning Prayer and Advice for a Rainbowdaughter

FOR THIS MORNING:

all around, the everything,
trees, horizons, waters, the animals,
and how one sees, hears, smells,
touches and tastes everything;
these all leading to humility,
> I make myself present,
> facing east.

Feed them, ask for strength, courage,
for it is all theirs,
> I make myself present,
> feeding them.

Beseech the worldspirit, ask for hope
for it comes from there,
> I make myself present.

Recognize the true power, say it
for that is the way,
> I am arriving to myself.

All around, the everything:
> make her all gentle,
> make her all beautiful,
> make her all humble,
> make her a true rainbow daughter,

traveling and seeking and learning and arriving
truly to herself, one with the earth mother
to whom she is kin.

Humbling ourselves, we thank you.

ADVICE:

learn how to make good bread, being careful and patient in everything
   you do, feeling your making, being gentle with the kneading and
   savoring the result;

enjoy yourself as a child, listen for sounds, let sights thrill you
   incredibly, but do not be demanding, inappropriately, of yourself or
   of others;

pray, in whatever fashion, but always with sincerity and with
   humility;

laugh, o child, learn to and let yourself laugh, always as a happy child
   for honestly enjoyable things;

learn how to recognize sadness, the small and large tragedies, coping
   with them by seeing them in their own true perspective so that you
   may appreciate your own;

respect your parents, brothers and sisters, all your kin, friends, and
   most of all yourself, learn this well;

this is not all, certainly not all, because there is so much more, and
   you will learn that.

Canyon de Chelly

Lie on your back on stone,
the stone carved to fit
the shape of yourself.
Who made it like this,
knowing that I would be along
in a million years and look
at the sky being blue forever?

My son is near me. He sits
and turns on his butt
and crawls over to stones,
picks one up and holds it,
and then puts it into his mouth.
The taste of stone.
What is it but stone,
the earth in your mouth.
You, son, are tasting forever.

We walk to the edge of cliff
and look down into the canyon.
On this side, we cannot see
the bottom cliff edge but looking
further out, we see fields,
sand furrows, cottonwoods.
In winter, they are softly gray.
The cliffs' shadows are distant,
hundreds of feet below;
we cannot see our own shadows.
The wind moves softly into us.
My son laughs with the wind;
he gasps and laughs.

We find gray root, old wood,
so old, with curious twists
in it, curving back into curves,
juniper, piñon, or something
with hard, red berries in spring.
You taste them, and they are sweet
and bitter, the berries a delicacy
for bluejays. The plant rooted
fragilely into a sandy place
by a canyon wall, the sun bathing
shiny, pointed leaves.

My son touches the root carefully,
aware of its ancient quality.
He lays his soft, small fingers on it
and looks at me for information.
I tell him: wood, an old root,
and around it, the earth, ourselves.

Baby Bird Prayers for My Children, Raho and Rainy

watching little birds learning
to fly, Spring 1975, SE Colorado

1
Gentle murmurs of wind, now,
be warm and soothing
to these little ones, this morning
and for all days of this world,
I offer my thoughts and prayers.

2
Be kind, sun, gentle.
I am yet small, my heart beats
with the fragile cycle of the universe.
Be kind, bright sun.
I feel your kindness upon me.
Make me grow tall and strong.

3
This morning, the rush
of my mother's wings
startles me.
Waking to coldness,
I shriek and I shriek.
The noises awaken me even more.
They penetrate to the hunger
I feel, and I shriek again.
My mother returns,
gently gliding into home.
She feeds me from her mouth.
She leaves, and I shriek
and I shriek again with love
and hunger and growing.

4
Protect these little things.
They are mere blood, bone,
muscle, and they are filled yet
with delicate dreams.
Their spirits are growing
and I want them to know
they come from the rhythm
that the universe is.
Please protect these little ones
and keep them and they will grow
well and rich with life.

5
Little fluff of feathers
alight softly unto the ground.
They welcome you, the soil,
the grass, the little seeds,
the countless insects.
You have fallen from the sky,
the trees, the white clouds.
Little Friends, they say.
You are welcome with us.
We are growing too
and we shall grow together.

6
Put your thoughts in mine,
your small hands, your dreams
with mine and walk with me.
I shall show you a few things.
I shall tell you a few names.
I shall keep you with me
for a while.
I will teach you
for a while.
And then you will fly.
You will fly.

Between Albuquerque and Santa Fe

I told a friend that I was writing what follows below. We were drinking some good red wine at his home on Cerro Gordo. His blondhair little daughter was crawling around. Once in a while his wife would rise from her chair and stir something in a pot. "Fine," Max said. I think I told someone else too but I forget who. It was a cold winter day, getting to evening. I had heard someone mention during that day that it would snow that night. "I think that's a good idea," he said.

FINGERS TALKING IN THE WIND

They talked,
laughed by making motions,
these children,
their voices.

The wind slowed down;
the Jemez and Sandia Mountains
shrieked their joy.

The children had gotten on the bus
in Santa Fe for Albuquerque,
about a dozen of them.

A Santo Domingo man
sat at the front of the bus.
He didn't say anything,
and he looked straight ahead.

Three teenage girls
from San Felipe Pueblo
were on their way home.
They giggled and laughed
and drank pop and ate cornchips.

I was on my way home.
All of us were on our way home.

One time, this friend who is a cowboy liked this girl very much. In fact, he loved her then. Another friend told me the story. This was during my friend's drinking period. One night, he got wild and lonesome. He went to the girl's house. She lived in a two-story house. With his lariat, he roped the chimney and hoisted himself up. All of a sudden, the girl heard a tapping on her bedroom window, and she looked and saw it was this guy. She laughed and let him in because it was cold outside and gave him a sandwich and some orange juice. Just like in the stories, that one. Don't ever tell him that one, though.

LIKE MISSISSIPPI

Several years back,
Shirley, Rand, Hilary,
Agnes, Brian, Raho and I
were on our way to Taos
just to look around, visit.

We were driving up
the La Bajada south of Santa Fe.
The clay is red there
and Shirley said,
"Just like Mississippi,"
and I said, "Yes, it is."

Further up the La Bajada
and looking west you can see
the land where a fence divides it.
One is Santo Domingo land;
the other side is a U.S. politician's.

One side is graybrown dry land
from overgrazing;
the other side is silvery
from replanting and money.

When you get to the top of La Bajada,
you can see the Sangre de Cristo,
the Jemez, the Ortiz,
and the Sandia Mountains.
They are all strong and silent.

That day, our two families
took photos as we held our arms
around each others shoulders.

This was the time I was a student at St. Catherine's Indian School in
Santa Fe, when we all went to pick apples in an orchard in Tesuque.
That was the first year I was ever away from home.

We all piled into large trucks in the morning and rode up there. It's
not too far. We picked apples and once in a while sneaked quick bites.
We laughed and joked and teased the girls. In the break before lunch,
the boys went into the hills and chased rabbits. My cousin almost
caught one.

We ran back down to the orchard when they called us for lunch. The
nuns gave us baloney sandwiches and lukewarm milk and apples for
lunch. We picked apples for a short while after lunch. And then be-
cause it was a tradition, all the boys ran back to the school.

It's about nine miles up a long, long hill, alongside the highway to
Santa Fe and then down a long downsloping ridge. All the way, there
are cedar trees and some piñon. When everyone got back to the school,
we all went into the chapel and said a prayer for thanks. That was
that time.

A NEW MEXICO PLACE NAME

In this case, American history
has repeated itself.
It is too easy to stop itself.

COCHITI CITY

The crux is a question
of starving or eating.
An unfair question, surely
but who of the people
will not find it necessary
to ask?

Salas, of the old city,

points his finger
toward the

CITY

off to the right,
pointing to where
there is a sacred place.
"Right there," he says,
a halting in his voice,
"right there,"
and a bulldozer rumbles
over the horizon
of the hill unto that place.

This year a model

CITY

is being sold by salesmen
from Southern California.
Sometimes I think
that history will come
to know no one
except its salesmen.

Sam, Jody, and I went to see the model city in June 1971. I had just
hitched back from North Carolina. Armed with a tape recorder
and questions, we went up there. Sam took a photo of the sign:
COCHITI CITY.

The U.S. Corps of Engineers were busy. Their heavy machines were
incessant. There were some pipelines and sprinklers in operation.
There was no grass in sight. The steel blades had taken care of that.
The ground was bone bare.

We went to the sales office and stood around, arrogant young men, anx-
ious and nervous, and then we asked for the manager. Someone led us
to his office. He stood up, smiling, cool, and shook hands with us and
invited us to sit down. Sam paced the floor like a mountain lion.

The man punched a button on his intercom and spoke into it. A pudgy
man came with a sheaf of brochures and forms under his arm. He

passed them all around. Sam refused the handout. We asked questions and Jody turned on his tape recorder. It was incongruous, of course. Three Indians, young and angry, bantering with two whitemen who represented millions of dollars from somewhere, asking insistent questions which had no chance, realistically, of being answered.

We stayed only as long as Sam could stand it—he paced all that time—and before he lunged at that smiling salesman. We laughed and tried to talk with a Cochiti man who was watering some shrubbery foreign to the land. One of the salesmen called to him and he went over and then around the corner of a building. A pretty Indian girl at the reception desk refused to talk with us. We left.

On the way from COCHITI CITY, we saw several Indian men digging at a big hole in the ground. We waved to them. Sam took a photo and said he would title it, "Indians Building a New Way of Life." We didn't wonder what was to fill in the hole. It wasn't a strange feeling at all that there wasn't much to say. We stopped at Pena Blanca for a half pint and a six-pack. On the way back to Albuquerque, we drank in silence.

BACK INTO THE WOMB, THE CENTER

We got into Dave's VW
in Albuquerque and drove
for Cochiti Canyon,

past the village, on a dirt road
onto a mesa which very gently
upsloped, and Dave pointed
to a distant white space of clay,
saying, "Right there is the beginning."

At the mouth
the canyon begins without notice.
It's just jumbles of rock.
The canyon walls become higher
and you don't notice at all
that you're going deeper in.

It's higher then,
you can tell by the oak

and soon the ponderosa.
The air is cooler
and suddenly there is a fish hatchery
and a couple of buildings
painted like the US Game & Fish Dept.
We passed on by, rising,

until about a mile up, again suddenly,
we came upon a small, clear dam
surrounded by huge boulders,
and we stopped.

I found that the dam
is a natural one,
caused by an ancient rockslide,
and then I looked up
and the immensity of the place
settled upon me without weight.
I knew that we were near
one of the certain places
that is the center of the center.
Later on, when I walked
a mile up, I found the crotch
where the canyon enters
the mountain, the crotch
where there is a clump
of thick brush, and I felt cold.

It is strange this time,
and I have to pray this way.
"Do you mind if I sit on this stone
and lean against this mountain
and listen to the silence of everything?
Do you mind if I go back 10,000 years?"

My mother and my father took me away to school that time. We got
on the train in Grants. My father worked for the AT&SFRY railroad at
that time, he had a pass which we could use to go most anywhere the
railroad went. This time it was to Santa Fe, but the railroad only got as
far as Lamy and from there we had to ride the bus into town.

The way we went was this way. From Grants past our home in Mc-Cartys where my mother said, "There's our home. Look." I looked but tears blurred my eyes, the train noise was heavy on my ears. And then Laguna, past Mesita, turning southeast for Belen where the train heads north for Albuquerque. From Albuquerque past the pueblos of Sandia, Bernallio, Algodones, San Felipe, and Santo Domingo. And then unto the Galisteo uplift from where you can see the largest mountains of the southern Rockies, the Sandias, Jemez, and the Sangre de Cristo. The train goes on the uplift until almost to Lamy where it flattens out and is like that until the train slows down and stops at the depot. We got out with a few other people and got on the bus for Santa Fe.

It was almost dark by then and became really dark by the time we got into the city. My father tried to cheer me up by telling funny stories of the time he went to school in Santa Fe. We stayed at the De Vargas Hotel that night. My father said he had to go get some cigarettes. It was during Santa Fe Fiesta that time. He was gone for two hours and when he came back I was still awake and he was singing under his breath and I could hear him talk soothingly to my mother.

The next morning we all walked up to the school. On the way up there my father bought us a bag of Nambe peaches and we ate them on the way. The nuns at Saint Catherine's Indian School seemed to be waiting for me and they patted me on my shoulder and said that Mass was about to begin. We all went into the chapel. During a lull in the service, when everything was quiet except for the priest moving silently about the altar, I fainted.

I just fainted, that's all, into the subtle chasm that opens and you lose all desire and control, and I fell, very slowly, it seemed. I found myself being carried out by my father to some steps in front of the boys recreation hall. He talked with me for a long time, slowly and gently, and I felt him tremble and stifle his sobs several times. He told me not to worry and to be strong and brave.

I wonder if I have been. That was the first time I ever went away from home. It's a memory of it, that time.

A Birthday Kid Poem

Don't worry about the pain
at the upper part of your hip.
Bone and flesh are ephemeral
in the count of centuries after all,
and your life is intermittent.

Prefer to consider eternity
at least; that way you know
that things continue the way
that life has been, a constant motion
gathering everything from the outer limits
of the universe—wherever those are—
into the core of the universe—
wherever that is—and all through the motion
which is time and sequences
you are passing through.

Consider that instead and love
yourself well and appropriately.
Love your children and love your kinfolk.
Love the mothers of your children.
Love the small things.
Love the big things.
Love things in the manner that they should be loved.
Be strong, humble, clear in vision,
and do not dream so fantastically
that you lose the reality
that dreams are,
that they are signals and roads
by which to guide the reality
of all the days that you are going through.

Believe that things will end well
for you; believe that things
will end well for all things.
Believe that hope is useful

even if sometimes it seems useless.
Believe, o man, o god, believe.

Be cool now.
Think of Coyote.
Think of Magpie.
Think of Raho Nez and Rainy Dawn.
Think of all the things you love.
Think peace and humility
and certainty and strength.

It shall end well.
It shall continue well.
It shall be.
It shall.
It shall.
It shall.
It shall.

That's the way things continue.
Emeh eh eh ka aitetah.
That's the way that things become.
Emeh eh eh naitra guh.

Quumeh.
Hahtrudzaimeh.
Like a woman.
Like a man.

Nyow skhetsashru.
Endure.
Nyuu skhetsashru.
Be enduring.
BE ENDURING.

HOW MUCH HE REMEMBERED

Woman, This Indian Woman

1
O, I miss you so lonely.
Aiiee, it aches.

The black mountain.
The black crow.
Long black hair.

She came riding
over a small hill,
from behind a cedar tree
and faced me.

Her eyes are deep,
the history
of long dreams,
into me.

A small creek by Tsaile,
a small girl
drives her sheep by.

It's so long a time,
a lonely word
without you,
alone.

2
Her brown hands touched
his face, the breath drawn
out from his life,
her hands trembling,
a last giving so close
to life it is near birth.

Eyes touch: lover, I remember
the quick lights moving.
Hair touch: man, my fingers
pushed smoothly upon.
Teeth touch: boy, I fed you
to grow, to run, to vibrate.
Face touch: Sun, it was I held
out my hands, my body to receive.

3
When she laid down,
she was conceived.

When she gave birth,
she was glad for her son.

When the boy asked,
she said, "The Sun, your Father."

When she died,
the earth remembered her well.

4
I remember her well.

Watching Salmon Jump

It was you:
I could have crawled
between mountains—
that is where seeds are possible—
and touched the soft significance of roots
of birth and the smell of newborn fish

        and

know how it is
leaping into rock
so that our children may survive.

Some Indians at a Party

"Where you from?"

Juneau
Pine Ridge
Sells
Tahlequah
Salamanca
Choctaw
Red Lake
Lumbee
Boston
Wind River
Nambe
Ft. Duchesne
Tesuque
Chinle
Lame Deer
Seattle

Pit River
Brighton Res
Vancouver
Parker
Acoma
the other side, ten miles from Snow Bird.

That's my name too.

Don't you forget it.

Places We Have Been

VADA'S IN CUBA, NEW MEXICO

I wrote her a small poem about this.
She sent me back a xerox copy, wrote,
"Thought you might like to have a copy."
I wouldn't mind having copies
of all the things I've ever done.

Vada's is a dark, cool roadside bar
on a slow spring day, hot outside.
We'd turned back this side of Nageezi,
been going somewhere we never got to,
and we stopped in for a drink.
I ordered a whiskey shot and beer,
and she was drinking beer.

Old man Chicano bartender there,
we liked him and he liked us.
He spoke German from the War,
and she spoke French. An old man Jemez,
friend of bartender, was there too.
He spoke Navajo. I spoke Acoma.
We were a confluence of separate languages
and the common language of ourselves.

We flipped a quarter for music
but the bartender said, "Forget it,"
smiled and put his coins in the jukebox.
She asked, "What are we going to do now?"
"I don't know," I answered.
Maybe we should go someplace.
Yeah, maybe. We drank up,
said goodbye to the old men,
"We'll see you again," and left.

I wonder how they all are
and where we went after we left.

NORTHERN MAINE

There was a mountain toward Canada.
I looked at the horizon it was
for a long time because I thought
it looked like Kaweshtima at home
and I had left a couple months back
and was lonely for my son and wife.

We'd driven on narrow roads from Calais.
I was glad they were deserted,
and we didn't stop for anything because
I was leery of the white people
being leery of me, a long-haired Indian.
We arrived finally at Moosehead Lake.
We walked on the lakeshore
until we got cold and hungry and found
we had nothing to eat. It was too far
to drive to a store seventeen miles back.
We had come that far, and it was too far
then to go back. We went hungry.

I watched her trying to photograph
a bare twig against the steel gray sky.
I was oblivious to her purpose,
and I watched the wind ripple the water
and imagined huge fish in the lake.

She looked at me then, and I helped her
jump ashore safely from a stone.

I woke late that night, late
to a bird cry from across the lake,
a far shore. I saw pine branches
against the black sky. It was too far
then into the night darkness, too far
away from the pinpoints of stars,
and I was too far away, alone.

INDIANHEAD BAY

I wrote a poem with Kennebek River
in it, wondering where the hell
all the Indians had gone to, no sign
of them around. Even I felt foreign.
I had commented, "Not even dried feces left."
Her father said, "There used to be some."

Whose Indian head?—I kept thinking.
Mine I suppose—I kept answering.

Her mother told her she thought I was lazy.
I liked to sleep late, nothing for a
Pueblo Coyote to do there, too far from home,
no sandstone cliffs to build dwellings upon.

We walked down to the Bay.
It scared me because it looked much deeper
than it was, the water moving too slow.
I could barely perceive the seaweed flowing.
I wondered how many Indians there had been.

She showed me a cabin her sister had built.
She was planning on building one too.

I helped her father rake dry brush together
on land he was clearing. It *was* strange,
an Acoma Indian helping a Pilgrim descendant
pile underbrush together to burn.

My head probably as I said.

ITHACA, NEW YORK

On the way to Buffalo we got lost.
I got lost a lot that year.
A night freeway this time,
I remembered Vada's, and I asked,
"How far?" "I don't know," she said.

We found a junction bar, a hotel
upstairs, low sleek cars parked outside.
We walked in, asked for a room,
and the hotel night clerk wondered
at us for a long moment, not knowing
what to think of a long-haired Indian
with a white woman asking for a room
at a Black hotel. Tired, I was going
to explain, "I'm just taking her back
to her ship, man, that's all,
give us a damn room."

An ancient elevator took us
to a bare gray room.
I kept worrying about being lost,
kept looking out the window.
"You promised," she said, trying
to reach me. "I know," I said and went
on ahead on a far and wearied bourbon
trip to sleep.

UPSTATE

Coming from Montreal,
we stopped at a roadside place.
She had to use the restroom
and I stepped into the tavern.
A man, surly white drunk, told me,
"I know an Indian who dances nearby."
He wanted to show me, cursed me
because I was sullen
and didn't want to see.

She came and saved me.
I said, "It's a good thing you're white."
And she was hurt, angry.
It's an old story.
On the wall was a stuffed deerhead,
fluff falling out, blank sad eyes.
We drove madly out of the parking lot,
and she didn't say anything
until we finally arrived in Vermont.

We were tired of being in the car,
our bodies and spirits cramped.
We ate in a small town.
We drove to a hillside.
The weather was muggy and hot.
I talked crummy to her, made love,
she cried, I felt sorry and bad.
I get crazy sometimes and impossible
I've heard.
        It rained hard that night.
The lights of the town below
shimmering through the rain into me.
All night long, I was lonely
and bothered by New England Indian ghosts.

How Much Coyote Remembered

O, not too much.
And a whole lot.

Enough.

Morning By A Lakeside In Marion County, S.C.

Spring 1970

1

Dear Kathryn and the others,
the young makers and builders
who are called, by them, the anarchists:

I was driving the highway between Pensacola & Atlanta,
not paying much attention to the car radio at all
until on a stretch of dull Interstate asphalt,
a voice shattered boredom like a howitzer.

I stopped and was silent and felt sorrow
eventually, just past a sign which read:
NO PARKING EXCEPT IN CASE OF EMERGENCY.
I climbed a fence and hugged a tree, hoping
to receive forgiveness by loving the earth.

Was it a good place to die,
someplace called Kent State USA?
What period of history is this anyway?

2

Last night old Bullfrog was trying
to make up his mind about his bass,
whether to keep it or throw it away.
Tuning it one last time, all night long.

It's hard to throw old things away.
In the morning, bass strings trembly
and loose, he still hasn't made up his mind.

3

In all my life I never thought
I would spend a night in South Carolina.
But here I am, Marion County. Sandy land
planted with cotton, some soybean, tobacco.
I've seen the white people
and I've seen the Black people.

The whites mainly driving cars,
the Blacks mainly walking.
I've seen the worn gray shacks
and I've seen the ranchstyle homes.
Marion seems like a clean town.
I've even seen a sign reading,
"We always mind our own business."

4
The sun comes red out of clouds
at the far end of the lake.
"Good words and love," Jackson said
in east Texas, talking
about the Alabama-Coushatta way
of saying goodbye.

"We came here," he said, laughing
bitterly, over a case and half of Schlitz,
"in the 1800's. Before that
we owned Georgia, Alabama, and Mississippi."

Woman Dreamer: Slender Oak Woman

A pretty girl lent me some typing paper.
Long ages of Indian in her face; this one
from the north. San Luis Valley, family
of farm workers; beets, onions, lettuce.

At lunch in the line, there was a Mexican
woman pushing a cart of hot food.
She was very dark, high bones in her face,
flashing dark eyes, scar on her upper lip.

   I can imagine you, woman,
    woman, when you were fourteen,

running toward the mountains.
You must have had long legs,
slender oak, running running
in the wind.

There was another woman I saw in the main
VAH office building. She was drinking
water from the fountain, and later I saw her
walking. She reminded me of a woman
I loved for fun. She moved like she laughed,
very sure of herself, teasing, long legs.
She was salmon; fast runner; she was oak
slender woman; Tlingit.

I can see the oak slender
woman running the mountainslopes.
The wind flies into her.
The sky is clear all the way
to all the horizons.
She, the slender oak young spring
of herself, is running running.

Apache Love

*Cibecue is on the western edge
of the White Mountain Apache
land in Arizona*

It is how you feel
about the land.

It is how you feel
about the children.

It is how you feel
about the women.

It is how you feel
about all things.

Hozhoni,
in beauty.

Hozhoni,
all things.

Hozhoni,
for all time.

Hozhoni,
through all journeys.

"Those are our White Mountains," Judy said.

"Don't let these old women do all the work for you,"
old man said.

"It makes me feel good, all you young people,"
old woman said.

"It is our own Apache way," Mrs. Early said.

If I ever come back,
it will be through here.

It would be good to ride a horse
through these mountains.

It would be good to stop and rest
by a stone as big as the spirits.

It would be good to go back
and touch the Mountain's people.

Salt River Canyon,
"It's about fifteen miles," Sam said.

Salt River Canyon,
we threw stones into the canyon.

Salt River Canyon,
the mountains, the canyons all around us.

Apache old woman, gray hair, you in beauty.

Apache woman, black hair, you in beauty.

Apache young girl, strong limbs, you in beauty.

Apache younger girl, growing, you in beauty.

It is you,
it is you,
it is you,
it is you.

Her Story About Saving Herself

The way she tells it
makes me feel wealthy,
thinking about a woman,
her child growing in her,
determined to save herself
by going into the Minnesota woods
to build a home.

    Are you Wolverine Woman?
    Are you the luminescence
    that spirits away when I smile,
    recognizing you?

I see her the way
that warmth comes over me
gradually as she dispels
with her words any doubts
I ever had about my life.
Her story holds me true,
and I want to keep on
listening and hearing
and knowing her tell me again.

    Later, Wolverine Woman,
    the moon will be out
    and the silver shadows
    will stand still for me.

Two Coyote Ones

I remember that one about Coyote
coming back from Laguna Fiesta
where he had just bought a silver belt buckle.
He was showing off to everyone.
That Coyote, he's always doing that,
showing off his stuff.
                              Probably,
it wasn't as good as he said it was,
just shiny and polished a lot.
I never saw it myself, just heard about it
from one of his cousins who said
the Navajo was kind of wobbly when Coyote
bought it for five dollars and a small sack
of wheat flour he'd "borrowed"
from a Mesita auntie.
                              That Coyote,
I wonder if he still has that silver buckle
that everyone was talking about
or did he already pawn it at one of those
places "up the line."
He's like that you know and then he'd tell
people who ask,
                              "Well, let me tell you.
I was at Isleta and I was offered
a good deal by this compadre who had
some nice ristras of red chili. He had
a pretty sister . . ." and so on.
And you can never tell.

One night in summer in southern Colorado,
I was sitting by my campfire.
Rex, the dog, was lying down
on the other side of the fire.
                              I could see
the lonely flicker of the fire
in his distant eyes.

(That sounds like just talk
but Rex was a pretty human dog.)
                                    And this
blonde girl came along. I mean that.
She just came along, driving a truck,
and she brought a cake.
That was real Coyote luck, a blonde girl
and a ginger cake. We talked.
She lived south of my camp some miles,
just past the bridge over the Rio de la Plata.
Her parents and her brothers raised goats.
That's where the money was she said,
and besides goats are pretty-well mannered
if you treat them right.
                        I said, Well
I don't know about that. We used to raise
goats too.
            Coyote doesn't like goats too much.
He thinks they're smartass and showoff.
Gets on his nerves he says.
Goats think pretty much the same of him,
saying,
        Better watch out for that cousin.
He gets too sly for his ownself
to be trusted. He'll try to sell you
a sack of flour that's got worms in it
that somebody probably has thrown out.
                                        And
they'd get into a certain story
about one time at Encinal when he brought
a wheelbarrow that was missing only one wheel
to this auntie he liked and he had a story
for why the wheel was missing . . .
And so on.

Anyway, the girl was nice, her hair shining
in the firelight, gentle soft voice.
She told me her name but I forget now.
Said she was going to Boston for med school,

said she liked raising goats but it was time
for her to go East.
                    Actually, we just talked
about the goats and what I was doing
which was living at the foot of the La Plata
Mountains and writing.
                    I think I could have
done something with that gimmicky-sounding
line, which was true besides, but I didn't.
It was just nice to have a blonde girl
to talk with. I had to tell Rex the dog
to cool it a couple of times. He and I
were alone a lot that summer, and we were
eager but we kept our cool.
When she was leaving I asked her to come
back again. She said she'd like to but
she was leaving for Denver the next day.
Okay then, I said and thanked her
for the ginger cake and the talk.
"Goodbye and goodluck." Yeah, "Goodbye."

There's this story that Coyote was telling
about the time he was sitting at his campfire
and a pretty blonde girl came driving along
in a pickup truck and she . . . And so on.

And you can tell afterall.

WILL COME FORTH
IN TONGUES AND FURY

A Designated National Park

Montezuma Castle in the Verde Valley, Arizona.

DESIGNATED FEDERAL RECREATION FEE AREA
ENTREE FEES
$1.00 FOR 1 DAY PERMIT
MONTEZUMA CASTLE ONLY INCLUDES PURCHASER
OR OTHERS WITH HIM IN PRIVATE NON-COMMERCIAL
VEHICLE
$0.50 FOR 1 DAY PERMIT
MONTEZUMA CASTLE ONLY INCLUDES PURCHASER
IN COMMERCIAL VEHICLE

AUTHORIZED
BY THE LAND AND WATER CONSERVATION FUND
ACT OF 1965

This morning,
I have to buy a permit to get back home.

Birds,
they must have been,
these people.
"Thank you for letting me come to see you."
I tell them that.

Secreted in my cave,
look at the sun.
Shadows on sycamore,

a strange bird and a familiar bird.
River, hear the river.
What it must be,
that pigeon sound.

Hear
in my cave, sacred song.
Morning feeling, sacred song.
We shall plant today.

PRESS BUTTON

(on a wooden booth)
                "For a glimpse into the lives
                of these people who lived here."

Pressing the button, I find
painted sticks and cloth fragments
in a child's hand,
her eyelashes still intact.
Girl, my daughter, my mother,
softly asleep.
They have unearthed you.

59TH CONGRESS OF THE UNITED STATES OF AMERICA
AT THE FIRST SESSION,
BEGUN AND HELD AT THE CITY OF WASHINGTON
ON MONDAY, THE FOURTH DAY OF DECEMBER,
ONE THOUSAND, NINE HUNDRED AND FIVE.

AN ACT
FOR THE PRESERVATION OF AMERICAN ANTIQUITIES.

And a last sign post quote:

BUILT SOMETIME BETWEEN
1200 AD AND 1350 AD
ABANDONED BY AD 1450.

s/ The Sinagua Indians

SEE MUSEUM FOR MORE INFORMATION

Long House Valley Poem

the valley is in northeastern Arizona
where one of the largest power centers
in this hemisphere is being built

Sheep and woman.
The long brown and red land
looming unto the horizon.
                Breathe in so deeply.

Tsegi,
a canyon.
"Hello" and "Goodbye,"
but always Hello
and smile.

The old rocks, millions of years old.

A Mohawk camper trailer
pulled behind a big white Cadillac.
Tourists,
the crusaders.

A cop car
flashing frenetic orange.
Slowwww down. I can't
even remember my license plate number.

And then, suddenly
the Peabody Coal Company.
Black Mesa Mine.
Open pit.

Power line over the Mountain,
toward Phoenix, toward Denver,
toward Los Angeles, toward Las Vegas,
carrying our mother away.

A sign reads: Open Range.
Bulldozer smoke and dust rise
from the wounded Mountain.

A PLAGUE ON ALL YOUR DAMN HORSEPOWER
A PLAGUE ON YOUR KENNECOTT COPPER BLIGHTS

The old rocks, millions of years old.

Horses quietly grazing, quietly.
A skinny black one throws his head
at the sky, at the wind.

The Yei
and hogans and the People
and roadside flowers
and cornfields and the sage
and the valley peace,
they are almost gone.

Blessings

for Mrs. Aguilar, James, and my son
at a civilrights fundraising function
in 1969

You and your crooked leg, James.
You and your hunger, Mrs. Aguilar.
They are getting bored with your misfortunes.

My son is too young to talk
about what his bones need or how much his
belly might be hurting,
but I am thinking they will be bored
with him too.

"How much gas do you need for a tractor?
For three tractors?" they ask.
"How much would it cost our foundation?"

I wait for them to ask,
"How many dreams have you spent lately?
How many hopes?"

We are not hungry for promises of money
nor for anyone to write us
carefully written proposals.
We are hungry for the good earth,
the deserts and mountains growing corn.
We are hungry for the conviction
that you are our brothers and sisters
who are willing to share our love
and compassionate fingers in your hands.

The grass of this expensive lawn
and the drinks make me feel
a stranger and my acute hunger.
My son smiles while someone says,
"I am not politic; I am talking with you."

Mrs. Aguilar with your orange dress
and plastic flowers, I am asking blessings
for you with prayers for corn and potatoes,
the growing things for your land,
and my son is hoping with his smile
not to be hungry tomorrow.

James, you 1950's pachuco,
you are aching in my throat.
You are the many Indians, the anarchists
rising out of the wine slop, angry,
the ones killing false promises,
fighting cops—we are also seeking
blessings for you, for us, for our children
in this war.

Irish Poets on Saturday and an Indian

We bought each others' drinks,
talked poetry, talked about Welch,
Blackfeet from Montana, good poet,
that Indian chasing lost buffalo
through words, making prayers
in literary journals. Yeah,
strange world, drinking bourbon
and water and then beers. Tony,
one Irish poet, and Sydney,
the other Irish, who laughs deeply
at a name Tony says. Murphy,
Murphy Many Horses, laughing Irish
whiskey Indian, we laugh for the
sound of our laughter.
            And then,
I tell about the yet unseen translation
where Indians have been backed up into
and on long liquor nights, working
in their minds, the anger and madness
will come forth in tongues and fury.

Ten O'clock News in the American Midwest

Bernstein disc jockey tells
about Indians on the ten o'clock news.
O they have been screwed.

I know everybody talks
about Indians yesterday,
the murdering conquest,

the buffalo bones strewn
across hills in Kansas,
the railroad roaring progress.

Late today or early tomorrow
in ghost dance dreams, surely,
we will find Bernstein doesn't know
what Indians say these days
in wino translations.
He doesn't know that.
And even Indians sometimes
refuse to know, because we fear
the trains and what Bernstein tells us
on the ten o'clock news.

Grants to Gallup, New Mexico

Grants, Okie town,
Texans from the oilfields
come to dig uranium
for Phillips Petroleum.
Milan, mobile home town.
    West,
      semis busting gut, gears snarling.
Sawmill this side of Prewitt.
    West for California.
Thoreau, gas station and bar.
Navajos leaning on the walls.
    West, pass on by,
      see you on the way back.
Top of The World,
Real Indian Village,
reptiles, moccasins, postcards 5¢,
restrooms, free water.
Coolidge.

Continental Divide.
North Chavez.
Iyanbito, a Shell Oil Co. Refinery.
    West, you see
    Red Gods emerging from the cliffs
    several miles north
    of the Santa Fe railroad.
    Keep going.
Wingate Army Depot, ammo storage
on the hills, rows and rows
of bunkers, freight cars pulling away
loaded for war, for Vietcong.
    West. A Cadillac
    with a fat white cat
    and a blonde teenybopper.
Church Rock turnoff
where an Indian man waits.
We stop for him and he runs to us.
Where you going?
Gallup.
    West. California is too far.
    Once, I been to California.
    Got lost in L.A., got laid
    in Fresno, got jailed in Oakland,
    got fired in Barstow,
    and came home.
Gallup, Indian Capital of the World,
shit geesus, the heat is impossible,
the cops wear riot helmets,
357 magnums and smirks, you better
not get into trouble and you better
not be Indian. Bail's low though.
Indian Ceremonial August 7–10,
the traders bring their cashboxes,
the bars are standing room only
and have bouncers who are mean,
wear white hats and are white.
    West, sometimes I feel like
    going on.
    West into the sun at evening.

The following words are for a white friend who I was
telling about the time, day before New Year's, 1972, that
I helped a Jemez man off the pavement where he had
fallen. The words, also, are for that Jemez and for me.

I find now
that you have finally
come to know me

or so you say

when I have
followed you
all this time,
following your guilty tracks,
finding all those bodies
strewn along the way.

I have honestly loved
your women,
even been insulted by them,
even as they asked
for forgiveness
trying to prove you guiltless.

Now, you have found me,
shorn naked and ashamed,
cold and shivering,
sprawled at this one corner
of your trackless
American concrete patterns.

I welcome you
anyway and again
to see into me
in order that you may see
yourself.

"And The Land Is Just As Dry"

line from a song by Peter LaFarge

The horizons are still mine.
The ragged peaks,
the cactus, the brush, the hard brittle plants,
these are mine and yours.
We must be humble with them.

The green fields,
a few, a very few,
Interstate Highway 10 to Tucson,
Sacaton, Bapchule,
my home is right there
off the road to Tucson,
before the junction.
On the map, it is yellow
and dry, very dry.
Breathe tough, swallow,
look for rain and rain.

Used to know Ira, he said,
his tongue slow, spit on his lips,
in Mesa used to chop cotton.

Coming into Phoenix from the north,
you pass by John Jacobs Farm.
Many of the people there,
they live in one room shacks,
they're provided for by John Jacobs.
Who pays them $5 per day in sun,
enough for quart of wine on Friday.
Ira got his water alright.
Used to know him in Mesa in the sun.
My home is brown adobe
and tin roof and lots of children,
broken down cars, that pink Ford
up on those railroad ties.
Still paying for it
and it's been two years since

it ran, motor burned out,
had to pull it back from Phoenix.

Gila River, the Interstate sign says
at the cement bridge over bed
full of brush and sand and rusty cans.
Where's the water, the water
which you think about sometimes
in empty desperation?
It's in those green, very green fields
which are not mine.

You call me a drunk Indian, go ahead.

Vision Shadows

Wind visions are honest.
Eagle clearly soars
into the craggy peaks
of the mind.
The mind is full
of Sunprayer
and Childlaughter.

Mountain dreams
about Pine brother and friends,
the mystic realm of boulders
which shelter
Rabbit, Squirrel, and Wren.
They believe in the power.
They also believe
in quick Eagle death.

Eagle loops
into the wind power.
He can see a million miles
and more because of it.

All believe things
of origin and solitude.

But what has happened
(I hear strange news from Wyoming
of thallium sulphate. Ranchers
bearing arms in helicopters.)
　　　to these visions?
I hear foreign tremors.
Breath comes thin and shredded.
I hear the scabs of strange deaths
falling off.

Snake hurries through the grass.
Coyote is befuddled by his own tricks.
And Bear whimpers pain into the wind.

Poisonous fumes cross our sacred paths.
The wind is still.
O Blue Sky, O Mountain, O Spirit, O
what has stopped?

Eagle tumbles dumbly into shadow
that swallows him with dull thud.
The sage can't breathe.
Jackrabbit is lonely and alone
with Eagle gone.

It is painful, aiiee, without visions
to soothe dry whimpers
or repair the flight of Eagle, our own brother.

Heyaashi Guutah

The diaphanous morning cloud
　　　　　　　　　comes
　　　　　　　　　　　down

from the southwest mesa
from Aacqu

and into Tsiahma,
passes,
and heads up the wet black road
to Budville.

> Poor wrecking yard,
> Baptist Indian Mission,
> tilted sign dangling
> over the door to Kings Bar.

That man stumbles
against the lurch in his belly.
The night's terrored sleep
is a reflection in the dark window.
Mud from the ravine
clings to his pants.

> It's not open yet.

Across the road, a woman waits.

The ghost moves slowly northward
toward Kaweshtima.
It looks back
and waits for them, patiently.

Time to Kill in Gallup

City streets
are barren
fronts for pain
hobbles toward
Rio Puerco wallow hole
           under the bridge.
My eyes are pain,
"Yaahteh."

Yesterday
they were visions.
Sometimes my story
has worked
but this time
       the falling scabs
reveal only a toothless
woman.

Gumming back sorrow,
she gags on wine.
One more countless time
       won't matter.
Says,
"One more,
my friend."
I know him, standing,
by the roadside.
He got lost,
"Didn't wanna go home,"
       and we left him
a ghost to remember.
Only sorrow has no goodbyes.

These Gallup streets
aren't much
for excuses
       to start on at least
one last good time.

"So forgetful,"
it's easy, "you are,"
she said.
       Sweeping her hand,
knocking on cold railroad tie.
She shudders
too often a load
of children bound
to be bound
in rags.

The children
have cried too many times,
would only dig more graves,
lean on church walls.
For warmth,
"Sure why not."
Look for nickels, dimes,
pennies, favors,
                quick cold kisses.
The child whimpers
pain
into gutters.
These streets never
were useful
for anything
except tears.

She rubs her one last eye.
The other is a socket
for a memory
she got ripped,
ripped off
at Liberty Bar,
saving a pint of wine,
thinking she was saving
grace
and would be granted
redemption
if she fought
or turned over
                one more time.

Sister. Sister. These streets
are empty.
They have only told sighs
which are mean
and clutch with cold evil.

There are no pennies
or favors left, no change.
But might be if we ask for keeps.

There is change.
We must ask for keeps.

> I will come back
> to you for keeps
> after all.
> I will, for your sake,
> for ours.
> The children will rise.

She walks on.
The streets are no longer
desperation.
The reeking vapors
become the quiet wind.
It rains at last.

You can see
how the Chuska Mountains favor
her dreams
when she walks toward them.
Her arms and legs unlimber.
All her love is returning.

The man she finds
is a roadside plant.

She sings then,
the water in her eyes
is clear as a child,

> of rain.
> It shall.
> It shall.
> It shall.
> It shall
> be
> these gifts
> to return
> again.

It will happen again, cleansing.

The People will rise.

For Our Brothers: Blue Jay, Gold Finch, Flicker, Squirrel

Who perished lately in this most unnecessary war, saw them
lying off the side of a state road in southwest Colorado

They all loved life.
            And suddenly,
it just stopped for them. Abruptly,
the sudden sound of a speeding
machine,
and that was it.

Blue Jay. Lying there,
his dry eyelids are tiny scabs.
Wartstones, looking ugly.
His legs are just old sticks
used to push ashes away.
O goddammit, I thought,
just lying there.
Thought of the way he looks,
swooping in a mighty big hurry,
gliding off a fence pole
into a field of tall dry grass,
the summer sunlight catching
a blade of wing, flashing
the bluegreen blackness,
the sun actually black, turning
into the purest flash of light.
And so ugly now, dead.
And nobody knows it except
for those black ants crawling
into and out of decaying entrails.
Nobody but those ants,
and I ask them to do a good job,
return Blue Jay completely
back into the earth,
back into the life.

Gold Finch, I took four tiny feathers
from your broken body.
I hope you were looking at me then
out of that life, perhaps
from the nearest hills,
from that young cottonwood tree.
I hope you blessed me.
Until I looked very closely,
I didn't see the fading blood stain
on a wing tip, and I sorrowed for you.
I have always been one to admire
the yellow, the color of corn pollen,
on your tiny feathers as I've seen
you glittering from branch to branch,
whirring and rushing from one tree
to another. I have seen the yellow
of your tiny body and the way
the shades of the cottonwood
and my grandfather's peach trees
could hide you so well
but in a moment your voice
would always speak
and you could be found.
Gold Finch. A pollen bird
with tips of black, flits
his head around and sings
reasonably pretty and revealing.
There you were, forgotten too,
the hard knots of gravel around
and under you, lying besides
the poorly made, cracked asphalt
road upon which sped that hunk
of steel, plastic and chrome.
Well, I'm sorry for the mess.
I'll try to do what I can
to prevent this sort of thing
because, Gold Finch, goddammit,
the same thing is happening to us.

Flicker, my proud brother.
Your ochre wings were meant
for the prayer sticks.
Askew.
Head crushed.
Misshapen.
Mere chips of rotting wood
for your dead eyes.
Crushed.
Askew.
You always were one to fly
too close to flat, open ground.
Crushed.

Squirrel, a gray thing
with bits of brown
where tiny ears join its head.
Eats seeds, nuts, tender roots,
tiny savory items.
Runs quickly, flashing gray
and sudden.
Throws its head with jerky
nervous motion.
Flicks hardwood shrieks of sound.
Lying by the side of Highway 17,
staring with one dim eye across
the road at underbrush oak,
its body swollen with several days
of death in the hot sun,
its tail a distorted limp twist.
I touch it gently and then try
to lift it, to toss it
into some high grass,
but its fur comes loose.

It is glued heavily
to the ground with its rot
and I put my foot
against it and push it
into the grass, being careful
that it remains upright
and is facing the rainwater
that will wash it downstream.
I smell the waste
of its disintegration
and wipe its fur on my fingers
off with a stone
with a prayer for it
and murmur a curse.

I don't have to ask who killed you.
I know, and I am angry and sorry
and wonder what I shall do.

This, for now, is as much as I can do,
knowing your names, telling about you.
Squirrel. Flicker. Gold Finch. Blue Jay.
Our brothers.

---

*"The State's claim that it seeks in no way to deprive
Indians of their rightful share of water, but only to
define that share, falls on deaf ears."*

*an April 1974 editorial comment
in the Albuquerque Journal*

It was beloved old man Clay who used to say:

"It was in 1882, it was they came, and they said that they would mea-
sure up our land. They said it was to assure us of how much land we
owned. It was true that there were those of us who did not believe that
our concern was their purpose, and we did not want them here. But
they did send their men around our villages and our fields, and they

measured how much land there was, and sometime later—it didn't take
them very long—they told us what their findings came out to be and
that now we could rest assured that the land was recorded and filed
away in their government papers."

The cosmos is measured by American-made satellites, the land is be-
ing razed by Kennecott Copper and Anaconda Corporation monstrosi-
ties, and our land has been defined by the RIGHT OF WAY secured by
American RAILROADS, ELECTRIC LINES, GAS LINES, HIGHWAYS,
PHONE COMPANIES, CABLE TV.

RAILROADS

My father explained it to me this way,
"When the railroad was first built,
the land was drawn up into townships
and portions of the land were set aside
for schools, grazing, and public utilities.
And then we exchanged some land
with the railroads. They gave us land,
and we gave them some land."
It was only later I figured out that
"they" meant the USA which had given
the railroad the right of way
through our land and also allotted
them land so that what the railroad did
was "give" that land in exchange to us
who were the right of way.

When I was a ten-year-old altar boy,
there were photographs of the railroad
on the church sacristy walls.
They showed 1920 cars and men working
at laying track. There used to be
a watering stop for steam engines
near the church and the American man
who ran the pumps was named McCarty
and that's why the village, Deetseyamah,
I come from is called McCartys
on the official state maps.

ELECTRIC LINES

At first, the electric lines ran
only alongside the railroad tracks
but later they connected up the homes
in Deetseyamah and Deechuna with the lines.
Those electric lines connect up Aacqu
with America.

When they were putting up the lines,
there was this machine.
The machine had a long shiny drill
which it pointed at the ground
and drove it turning into the earth
and almost suddenly there was a hole
in the ground and the machine
drove on to another spot.
A couple of days later, a truck came
and threw long black poles
into the holes. At that age,
I didn't know much of anything,
and when my younger brothers and sisters
asked me what was going on
I probably told them some lie.

GAS LINES

The El Paso Natural Gas pipeline
blew up in the spring of 1966.
Old man Tomato told us what he was doing
on that early morning. He had just gone
out to piss outside his home
and had just come back inside
and was lying on his bed.
"I was singing a hunting song,
and then all of a sudden there was
this strange feeling and then I looked
out the window to the east and saw a light
over the hill beyond Dahska, but I knew
that it wasn't about to be dawn yet."

He told us that at the meeting in Acomita
where the El Paso Natural Gas man said
his company was sorry and they would
send money to make restitution very soon.

The El Paso Natural Gas company ran
through our best garden and left stones.
I was at Indian Boarding School at the time
and so I didn't see it coming through.
It wouldn't have made any difference
whether or not I'd seen it coming through
or whether we'd put a garden in that spring
because it would have come through anyway.
Nobody and nothing could stop it coming through.

HIGHWAYS

In 1952, the Felipe brothers led Nash Garcia
down U.S. 66 onto the reservation
and killed that State cop a few miles east
of Black Mesa. The State panicked
for a couple of months and the brothers
got sent to Federal pen for life.

One night during the Korean War,
my parents and I walked Eagle to the highway.
We stopped at Aunt Lolita's.
She had made some tamales and she put
them in a paperbag for Eagle to take along.
When we got to the highway,
Eagle showed me how to throw rocks sideways,
skipping them on the pavement to make sparks.
I had never seen that before.
My father flagged the Greyhound with a flashlight
and Eagle went off to Camp Pendleton and Korea.

When the Interstate was coming through,
a place where people had lived a long time
ago was uncovered. I carried one of my nephews—
he was just a kid then—on my back there once.
The old place had four kivas,

and there were many small rooms.
It was built beside a hill to the west
which protected it from the wind.
There was a wash to the east of their home.
When it rains the water flows from the north
onto a wide flat space.
The people planted there, on the south.

PHONE COMPANY

My cousin who was working for a uranium
mill and mine supply company at the time
won some prizes over the telephone.
The voice on the phone from the radio station
asked, "Who is the father of this country?"
He said, "Without thinking about it,
I answered, 'George Washington.'"

I don't think my Grandfather ever used
a telephone in his life although
he did see Eisenhower in Gallup once.
Ike was campaigning for President by train
and that was in the early 1950's.

When I was a boy, I didn't know
whether or not you could talk in Acoma
into the telephone and even after I found
that you could I wasn't convinced
the translation was coming out correctly
on the other end of the line.
I have to ask the telephone operators
to help. Direct dialing and long distance
information confuse me, and I think
telephone operators are exasperated with me even now.

CABLE TV

As far as I know, no one at Aacqu
subscribes to cable TV although CATV
from Grants has approached the people

with the idea, saying such things as,
"You can get thirty more channels than you do
presently. You can even get Los Angeles."
What kind of deal is that anyway?
Regular TV is crummy enough. My mother
used to watch "As the World Turns,"
and the kids are getting weird
from being witness to the Brady Bunch.

I don't know much about CATV
and I would like to think
that it's better that way,
but then I get this unwanted feeling
I better learn something about it.

RIGHT OF WAY

The elder people at home do not understand.
It is hard to explain to them.
The questions from their mouths
and on their faces are unanswerable.
You tell them, "The State wants right of way.
It will get right of way."

They ask, "What is right of way?"
You say, "The State wants to go through
your land. The State wants your land."
They ask, "The Americans want my land?"
You say, "Yes, my beloved Grandfather."
They say, "I already gave them some land."
You say, "Yes, Grandmother, that's true.
Now, they want more, to widen their highway."
They ask again and again, "This right of way
that the Americans want, does that mean
they want all our land?"

There is silence.
There is silence.
There is silence because you can't explain,
and you don't want to, and you know

when you use words like industry
and development and corporations
it wouldn't do any good.

There is silence.
There is silence.
You don't like to think
the fall into a bottomless despair
is too near and too easy and meaningless.
You don't want that silence to grow
deeper and deeper into you
because that growth inward stunts you,
and that is no way to continue,
and you want to continue.

And so you tell stories.
You tell stories about your People's birth
and their growing.
You tell stories about your children's birth
and their growing.
You tell the stories of their struggles.
You tell that kind of history,
and you pray and be humble.
With strength, it will continue that way.
That is the only way.
That is the only way.

I TELL YOU NOW

Waking

1
Woke early this morning,

        old morning moonlight.

Thought of visions,
dreams.
Not the past, not the future,

        just dreams.

Warm life coursing,
flowing through
the circle of everything,
tying me in:

        you're part of it all.
        Don't worry.

Drift back to sleep.

2
Woke
to a bird fluttering from the sky
through the tipi smokehole.

                    Startle

awake
and then smile.

It doesn't happen often.

Back through the smokehole a moment later.
Sent a prayer after it.

Thanks and humility.
All the way into the blue sky.
That is something,
how it happens.
"All the way into the sky."

My Father Singing

My father says,
"This song, I like it
for this one old man."
And my father moves
his shoulders, arms
and hands when he sings
the song.
My father says,
"When the old man
danced this song,
I like it for him."

This Occurs to Me

It has something to do
with intuition and instinct,
a mixture of appreciating
how the physical quality
of dirt and stone exist,
how useful they are,
what you can do with them.
Working with fingers, hands,
the mystery—knowing
it is not a mystery
that you can't possibly
know anything about—
that is yours.
Watching sparrows,
sheer cliff wall,
the effect of light and shadow,
line of stone mesa,
strata of sediment,
touching with foot and hand
the tamp of sand
against cliff wall,
noting the undershadow
of stone ledge.

All these, working in the mind,
the vision of weaving things
inwardly and outwardly
to fit together, weaving stone
together, my father tells me
how walls are built.

Uncle Jose

My sister, Myrna, said,
"Keithy didn't have an Acoma name
so I gave him one.
I called him Hishtiyani,
and I told Uncle Jose."
"'Hishtiyani, wah tawa eh
tchishratra,' he said."
Uncle Jose is over ninety.
He knows what good names are.
When he comes to visit, he asks,
"Ehku sthatyumu, Hishtiyani?"
And my sister goes looking
for his brother, Flint Arrowhead.

That time when my sister and I
were leaving our childhood,
Uncle Jose walked us home
late at night from the kiva.
It was very quiet.
When we got to my Auntie's home,
we found apples and oranges
strung together with yucca,
hanging from the door knob.
The next morning was the first day
after the four days had passed,
and we were allowed to eat salt again.

That Time

Agnes' aunt killed the goat.
I held it down, sitting on its belly.
I could feel its whole vibrating life,
the red blood, thinly spurting
in a low arc, and then just flowing.

Brian stood by, his childhands clutched.

Agnes' aunt is a gaunt, thin Navajo woman,
never married, takes care of Chee,
her dead sister's husband.

We skinned the goat, cleaned the guts,
and cut up the meat,
and saved the best parts for Chee.

We put the goat's head in the coals to cook
but the dogs stole it,
and it was half eaten before we found out.

We took the goat meat to a Squaw Dance.
Chee carried it under his arm in a sack,
and he wore his flatbrim hat and a new shirt.

That was that time.

When It Was Taking Place

This morning, the sun has risen
already to the midpoint of where
it will be at the center of the day.
The old man, Amado Quintana,
doesn't get up early anymore.

He still wakes early in the morning
but he can't see the clear things
in the dim light before the sun rises,
and he can't hear the clear sounds.
So he lies on his cot or he sits
in the wooden chair by the stove.
Sometimes he forgets he has not built
the fire in the stove and he wonders
why the weather has changed so early.

He is an old man.
The people in the village
call him Old Man Humped Back.
He has a hump on his back,
and the history about that
is he has lived a long time
and it has grown on him.

This morning at this moment,
Quintana is pointing to the river
below the hill on which he
and his grandson are standing.
He made his grandson help him
climb onto the hill and now
he is showing him the river
and the land before them.
The hill is not very high
and children climb it
to explore and look for things,
but from there you can see
the fields and the canals.

The old man cannot really see
those anymore; his eyes are cloudy
with a gray covering; the only thing
he can see is the sun when it is
at its brightest. Sometimes
he forgets, and he asks why
the weather has changed suddenly
and insists that it must be the times

and the people that are the cause.
But he can see in his mind,
and he tells his grandson,
"You can see the canal that runs
from that gathering of cottonwoods
and then turns to the south
by Faustin's field, that canal
was dug by the first people
who came down from the Old Place.
It was dug then."

He had been a child then,
and he played most of the time,
but he can remember his father
and the others with him.
They dug the canal from the river
to the east and turned it to the south,
and then it was easier
as the ground was softer
and the water found its own way.
They had worked and it was good.
They had talked a lot, laughed,
and they got so wearied.
At the end of the day, the men
drug themselves home,
and Amado can remember carrying
his father's handmade shovel
in his hands, and they would be
greeted at their home by his mother.

She would say, "Amo, my partner
and my son, have you worked so hard,"
and she would grab them and hold them
strongly to her.
She would especially make a fuss
over Amado who, at the time,
was their only child.
At that time, they lived in a low
windcarved cave with a wall of stones
along the front of it.

Amado Quintana can see that,
and he points it all out to his grandson,
and he wants him to see all those things,
and he tells the boy, "I was your age then
when it was taking place."

Poems from the Veterans Hospital

8:50 AM FT. LYONS VAH

The Wisconsin Horse hears the geese.

They wheel from the west.
First the unfamiliar sounds,
and then the memory recalls
ancient songs.

Sky is gray and thick.
Sometimes it is the horizon
and the sky weighs less.
The Wisconsin Horse cranes
his neck.
The geese veer
out of sight
past the edge of a building.

The building is not old,
built in 1937.
Contains men broken
from three American wars.

Less and less, the sound,
and it becomes
the immense sky.

TWO OLD MEN

November 1974

I've seen this old man around. Today as I was walking on the dike
ridge, I saw him at the edge of a marsh, looking for something. I won-
dered what. Had he lost something? Was he expecting to find some-
thing about yesterday in the autumn dry weeds and rushes in order
that he might insure tomorrow? I can only speculate. He has never
said a word that I have heard. Surely he speaks or has spoken in his
life but I have never heard.

I've seen you around.
Was it Iowa cornfield edge
or on the outskirts of Minneapolis?
It was late June I think.

Today, I saw you again.
You were moving through a tangle
of autumn rushes taller than you.
You moved so deliberately,
searching every stemmed shadow,
listening to the wind tremble
through the stubble.

You paused at the bottom
of an upslope—
from my distance the marsh
was a dark placid brooding
behind you—
and looked and looked.

What do you search for?
A glint of mica,
a shadow that needs no light,
an echo,
a bit of straw that tastes
of memory?

The old man's fingers dance a careful motion that has to do with
knowing the forms and designs that the eyes do not see, nor even the
mind, that mental acknowledgment is only a part, that in learning a

271

language or a sound, one has to "touch" the motion of what color is.
You have to not only see color but you must touch it, in a sense be-
come that color, know it, let it become part of you. I think that old
man knows. I like to watch him. He pushes his steel rim glasses with
bony knuckles back up the bridge of his nose. I call him Touching
Man.

He believes that colors
have shape, texture, substance,
depth, life he can touch.
I know they do.
I believe him.
When he is reaching
his long bony fingers
to a lettered sign
or a dark spot on the sidewalk,
there are the frankest features
of delight, surprise, wonder
in his face.

I believe him.

    Green has cold winter stems
the melted edge of snow
mirrors of angular gravel
see the grain of roots
moving my finger tips

    Chrome rainbows
on fire hydrant curve
meanings
no one sees vividly
by sight or mind
alone touching I see

    Form is not all
nor hearing
for the tensile mass
vibrates against
my tendrils
the mind that sprouts

and reaches into depths
the tips of my fingers

He touches me with the spider tendrils.
I would like to bring him a black rock
from the Lukachukai Mountains and give
it to him without telling him I have
given it to him.

Touching Man, you know things only
a very few know, and that is your strength,
your aloneness.

DAMN HARD

Today I remembered
the good buckhorn pocket knife I lost too.

She gave it to me as a surprise one day.
"What's this for?" I asked her.
I'd been drunk a couple of days before
and I wondered why.
"Oh, just because I wanted to," she said.

"I have loved you so damn hard and deeply,"
she wrote in a last letter.

The pocket knife must have cost
thirteen or fourteen dollars
and it felt good and heavy in the hand.

Dammit, I miss that feeling.

Today I told Joe, "I still feel crummy.
I almost went and bought one just like it
at a hardware store to replace it, but
it wouldn't have been the same thing,
something I lost."

"Yeah, I know," he said.

The other day we were talking,
sitting in front of Building 5.

"I'll never get that screwed up again
about a woman," Kenny said.
A bit later, a woman walked by,
her hips and thighs swinging.
Kenny shook his head and grinned big.
"But you know, it's damn hard not to,"
he said and, knowing, we all laughed.

Yeah, it sure is.

CHERRY PIE

We had barbecue beef on buns,
cole slaw with crushed pineapple,
coffee, and cherry pie.
Here in the VAH, at least,
America feeds well the men
it has driven mad.

"My favorite used to be cherry pie."

"Lemon is good too."

"When I was a kid at Indian School,
I worked cleaning yards on weekends.
Walking back to campus at evening,
I'd stop at this cafe on Fourth
and order banana cream pie.
Two slices of pie, boy, that was good."

Deanda hasn't been yelling lately.
They've been feeding him more
and better mind silencers lately.

Kelly offers his cole slaw.
Nobody wants it, shake their heads.
He offers his bread, we shake our heads.
"He's a dedicated nut," another nut says.

"The only pie I don't like
is mince meat, too rich."

"I wish I was rich."

"I almost married a rich girl once.
She was from Alabama."

There's always something that you almost
did that you should have done.

A cherry pie slips to the floor
off a man's saucer.
He stands there and everything is gone
from his face except sorrow and loss
and it's hard to lose those.

TEETH

After supper, Fuentes tells stories
about his teeth in front of Building 5.
With his gravelly voice, he says,
"Let me tell you guys.

"I used to have partials. Two teeth
and then four teeth. One night I was
with this girl. I put my four teeth
upon the dresser. Early next morning,
still dark, I was looking around
for the bottle, you know, feeling around
on the dresser, and all of a sudden
I heard this crunch under my shoe,
you know. It was my teeth, sonofagun.
I said, O what the hell, just teeth.

"Later on, I had another partial.
This time with six teeth. Me and some
other guys were drinking way back
in the hills above El Paso. We were
getting real low and one guy volunteered
to make a run. Fine. He said,
Let me borrow your coat, it's cold.
Sure, I said and gave him my coat.
I had put my teeth in that coat pocket,
sonofagun, and that guy is still on that run."

TRAVELING

A man has been in the vah Library all day long,
looking at the maps, the atlas, and the globe,
finding places.
                Acapulco, the Bay of Bengal,
Antarctica, Madagascar, Rome, Luxembourg,
places.

He writes their names on a letter pad, hurries
to another source, asks the librarian for a book
but it is out, and he looks hurt, and then he rushes
back to the globe, turns it a few times and finds
Yokohama and then the Aleutian Islands.

Later on, he studies Cape Cod for a moment,
a faraway glee on his face, in his eyes.
He is Gauguin, he is Coyote, he is who he is,
traveling the known and unknown places,
traveling, traveling.

SUPERCHIEF

Superchief left on Friday.
I didn't get a chance to see him
before he left but hope he's okay
and stays away from those morning bars
on Central Avenue and Fourth Street.

I saw him one time
up by the Nob Hill Shopping Center.
He had a small paper sack
of oranges and he was sitting
on the curb eating them.
His head was wobbling
from side to side.
He was trying to focus
on the asphalt in front of him.

A white woman watched him
a moment, standing behind him.
She moved on and then halfway
down the block, turned and looked
at him again, shook her head
not in sympathy or pity
but in contempt and disgust.

I tried to remember
his Acoma name as I walked away.
I walked down Silver and my feeling
of being useless was enormous.
I think I even wished my feelings
were as convenient as that woman's.

Even now I can feel
Superchief's withered gray eye
staring at the cement beneath his shoes.

ALONG THE ARKANSAS RIVER

I walk down to the river.
See four ducks,
two males and two females.
They swim away from me.
I stand very still watching them.

Two fly away then.
I decide to follow downstream.
The water eddies behind
the other two.

I don't follow too close
to the river's edge.
Instead I choose a path
through dry winter willow.

My god, I am lonely.
The sand is soft.
I wear tenny shoes.

A GOOD JOURNEY

Around a bend in the river
and upon a stretch of sand bar,
there are many ducks.
They don't seem to see me.
They are not alarmed.
I carry nothing in my hands.
They probably know.

I stand still,
and then I slip away
into the winter willow.

Wonder where Coyote is?
Probably in Tulsa by the bridge,
sitting on the grassy bank
near the University, hoping
she's gonna come along
after her three o'clock class
like she said she would.

A freight train was heading south.
Standing in a break of saltcedar
and willow, I got lonesome again.

That's probably where Coyote is.

LOOKING, LOOKING

This morning, looking
out the south windows of the Day Room,
I see Ralph standing on the loading dock again.
I call, "Ralph, hey," and he turns to the sound
of my voice two stories high, "Good morning.
What are you doing?"

He says something, points south,
past the dike ridge, the thickets
of spring saltcedar and willows, past
the Arkansas River and the cottonwoods.
He sweeps his hand in a motion
that is an awed gesture: All that land!

All that land! And he turns to me again
and says something and he grins,
pushes his fatigue cap back from his forehead.

"Which way is Taos?" I call.

He points to the southwest then.
Straight over the horizon of low hills.
Further on are the mountains, the mountains.
You just have to climb and then descend
on the other side.
He says things I can't hear, but I know.

"I'll see you later, okay?" I say.

Okay, he nods his head and waves his cap
and looks south again.
He keeps looking south, looking, looking.

FOR A TAOS MAN HEADING SOUTH

Thunder,
the sound from above,
the sound from below,
the sound from everything,
the sound from the rain,
thunder.

I hear thunder as I walk from the Print Shop
to the Canteen.
Thunder from the west and northwest.
The sky is dark with black clouds at the horizon.

The wind is humid and tree branches move slowly.

Rain will be welcome. It's been so long.
"It might rain," someone at Aacqu will say.
"Yes, it might rain."

Qow kutsdhe neh chah dhyuuh.
Hah uh, qow kutsdhe nehchah dhyuuh.
Let it rain.
Peh eh chah.

Mondragon is going home to Taos today.

"Hey, buddy, good luck now. Okay?
You be good and stay out of those deadly bars.
Okay?"

"Okay, yeah," he says.
It will be hard for him, but I believe him
when he says, Okay, yeah.
I have to. We have to keep believing in ourselves.

Yesterday, a white VA psychologist told us,
"I'm one-eighth Indian, but I don't make
a big deal of it," angry at us. "I wish you
weren't going back into the same environment."

Mondragon and I had to tell him, "That's our home,
our land, our people. That's our life. The life
of our people and land and home is who we are."

"You be good and strong, now, good buddy.
Come up to Aacqu. The people are having dances
in July, four days, when the katzina come.
Come visit. Bring your family."

"Okay. I'll come look you up," Mondragon says.

I wave and smile, trying to convey what strength
I have, the significance of my people,
of my belief in him and in myself to him.

Thunder,
the sound from above,
the sound from below,
the sound from everything,
the sound from the rain,
thunder.

Let this be your traveling prayer, Taos brother.
Good things come from below, from above,
from everything, from the rain.
Believe that.
Be strong now, be strong and good with yourself.

I Tell You Now

some things I wanted to tell an
Isleta woman walking by the Gizmo
Store, 2nd & Central, Albuquerque

I really have no words to match your stride.
You have two young children with you,
and they are probably your grandchildren.
I like the red flowered shawl over your head
and the starched lace on your wrists.
The Gizmo store, the yellowpaint walls,
plate window glass, and For Sale signs,
the cement pavement under your wornheel shoes—
all look out of place, even Albuquerque.

As I said, I really have no words which are equal.
Even the sheaf of stories I am carrying
under my arm to the printers, the stories
I did work carefully at, lack the depth
and the meaning of your walk.
O, I guess the words are adequate enough—
they point out American depredations,
the stealing of our land and language,
how our children linger hungry and hurt
on street corners like the ones I just passed,
but then I get the feeling that these
words of my youth are mere diatribes.
They remain useless and flat, when what I really wish
is to listen to you and then have you listen to me.
I've been wanting to tell you for a long time.

I tell you now.

A short time before my wife gave birth to our son, I went down to
your Pueblo to write a story for a newspaper for thirty dollars which
we needed. I talked with an older man. He was cleaning a horse corral.
I asked him about the huge tree by the railroad crossing. He said, "I
don't know how old it is. It's been there as long as I can remember."
He invited me to the San Augustine Fiesta the coming weekend. The
story I wrote was about the tree and the older man.

I like the story about the people handcuffing the Catholic priest, leading him to the edge of the village, and telling him never to come back. You know, the one with the German name who told you, the people, you were pagan and even had the earth of your church cemented over.

I like telling people that Isleta has the hottest chili along the Rio Grande.

Sometime ago, an American poet friend and I watched the people dancing in the plaza. He remarked, "Nowhere else in America can you see something like this." There were over a hundred dancers, young and old, and others were singing.

A longtime friend lives by the church. He's been around. Almost became a lawyer once, worked in Maine, Florida, even for the Indian affairs of the USA. Even was a hippie for a while, did a lot of dope, acted crazy and worried people, but I hope he's okay now.

The fight the Isleta people put up against the State when the State wanted to use your land for an Interstate was really something. The people turned the money down, told the State to go to hell, and the State got all pissed and frustrated. That was really something.

Once on the way home from the Army, I met an Isleta girl in Albuquerque; we spent two days in town before I thought I had better go home.

In El Paso, almost ten years ago, I met a man and woman and their three children. The man said they had relatives up north on the river and said some day they were going to visit because it had been a long time since they had come south.

One of the stories that's sort of funny but I don't like is about the pickle packing plant that failed, and the building is setting empty and useless now because the American government never meant for it to succeed.

I don't like the fact that one Fall a family was killed by a train at the crossing into the village because the AT&SFRY railroad never bothered to protect you when they laid their tracks through your land.

These few things then,
I am telling you
because I do want you to know
and in that way
have you come to know me now.

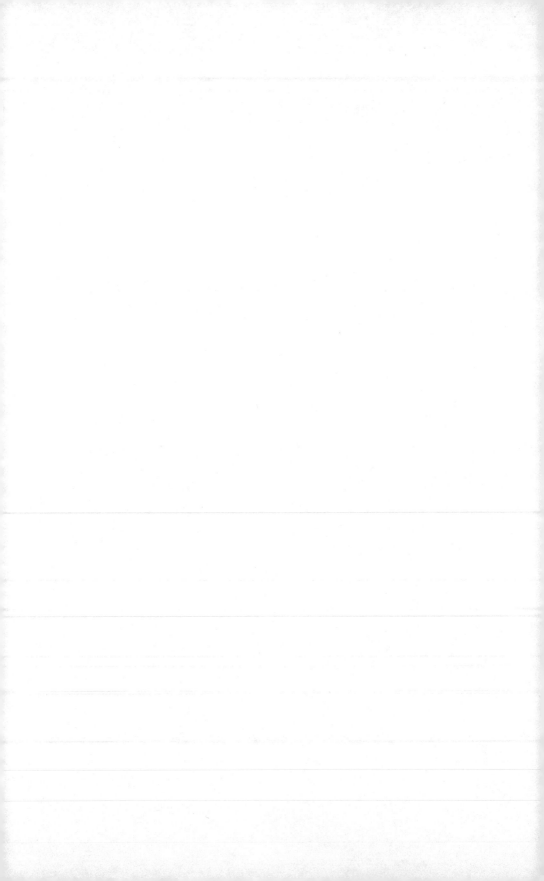

Fight Back: For the Sake of the People,
For the Sake of the Land

Hanoh Kuutseniah
Hahtse Kuutseniah

The songs, stories, poems and advice will always remember
my father, mother, and my people.

Now we know
what we must do.
Henah shrow uuh.

The land shall endure.
There will be victory.

The People shall go on.
We shall have victory.

Mid-America Prayer

Standing again
within and among all things,
Standing with each other
as sisters and brothers, mothers and fathers,
daughters and sons, grandmothers and grandfathers—
the past and present generations of our people,
Standing again
with and among all items of life,
the land, rivers, the mountains, plants, animals,
all life that is around us
that we are included with,
Standing within the circle of the horizon,
the day sky and the night sky,
the sun, moon, the cycle of seasons
and the earth mother which sustains us,
Standing again
with all things
that have been in the past,
that are in the present,
and that will be in the future
we acknowledge ourselves
to be in a relationship that is responsible
and proper, that is loving and compassionate,
for the sake of the land and all people;
we ask humbly of the creative forces of life

that we be given a portion
with which to help ourselves so that our struggle
and work will also be creative
for the continuance of life,
Standing again, within, among all things
we ask in all sincerity, for hope, courage, peace,
strength, vision, unity and continuance.

St. Louis, Mo.
May 1980

I TOO MANY SACRIFICES

My father passed on in spring 1978, returning back into the earth. He worked for the Santa Fe railroad company for twenty years or so, and he told my brothers and I to never work for the railroad and do the grueling labor he had to do in order to make a living.

I never worked for the railroad, but for a while I worked in the uranium mills and mines that opened up near home in the early 1950's. Many Acoma, Laguna, and Navajo people whose homeland is mid-northwest New Mexico worked in the underground and open pit mines, in the processing mills, and in the service industry in the nearby small towns, Grants and Milan.

The uranium extraction and processing industry in the Grants Mineral Belt, as the area is known, was massive. There were many social and economic factors, problems and issues, including racism, involved in working that land, our homeland. The following poem and story narratives speak for the sake of the People and for the sake of the land. Hanoh eh hahtse kuutseniah—the People's fightback is critical.

It Was That Indian

Martinez
from over by Bluewater
was the one who discovered uranium
west of Grants.
That's what they said.
He brought that green stone
into town one afternoon in 1953,
said he found it by the railroad tracks
over by Haystack Butte.
Tourist magazines did a couple spreads
on him, photographed him in kodak color,
and the Chamber of Commerce celebrated
that Navajo man,
forgot for the time being
that the brothers
from Aacqu east of Grants
had killed that state patrolman,
and never mind also
that the city had a jail full of Indians.
The city fathers named
a city park after him
and some even wanted to put up a statue
of Martinez but others said
that was going too far for just an Indian
even if he was the one who started that area
into a boom.

Well, later on,
when some folks began to complain
about chemical poisons flowing into the streams
from the processing mills, carwrecks on Highway 53,
lack of housing in Grants,
cave-ins at Section 33,
non-union support,
high cost of living,
and uranium radiation causing cancer,
they—the Chamber of Commerce—pointed out
that it was Martinez
that Navajo Indian from over by Bluewater
who discovered uranium,
it says so in this here brochure,
he found that green stone over by Haystack
out behind his hogan;
it was that Indian who started that boom.

Indians Sure Came in Handy

There was a Greek
who was the city judge
in the late 1950's and early 60's,
and he got in early
on the uranium boom business.

The workers were trying to organize then,
you know.
A lot of them had come in,
miners from West Virginia, Montana,
Colorado, oilfield workers
from Oklahoma, Texas, Louisiana.
The mines were pretty dangerous, wet,
water a foot deep most of the time,

and the companies said
there just wasn't enough timbers
to go around; there were cave-ins.
The companies just couldn't mine fast enough
to keep up with the demand
for yellowcake the Atomic Energy Commission
was buying and stockpiling then.

The mine superintendents
and the city judge,
who was also with the Chamber of Commerce,
were all good friends, of course.
They played golf at the Zuni Country Club.

During that organizing time
and during that strike in 1961,
that jail full of Indians sure came in handy.
The jailer would even call in sick for you
and tell you which mines were hiring Indians.
The unions didn't have much of a chance,
and Grants just kept on booming.

Starting at the Bottom

The truth is,
most of us didn't know
much about the unions
at any rate.
A job was a job.
You were lucky to have one
if you got one.
The truth is,
the companies didn't much care
nor did the unions,
even if both of them
were working our land.

When the mines came
to the Laguna and Acoma land,
the men and their families were glad
in a way because
the men wouldn't have to go
so far away to work
for the railroad in Barstow,
Richmond, Flagstaff, Needles.
Or to pick beets and onions
in Idaho, Utah, and Colorado.
Or work for the Mormons
in Bluewater Valley
who paid you in carrots and potatoes.

When Jackpile opened up
on Laguna land, some Laguna men got on alright,
at the bottom.
You have to start at the bottom, personnel said,
for a training period and work your way up.
The Acoma men went to the Ambrosia Lake mines
and always got stuck by the space
on the application forms
for previous mining experience,
but the mine steward explained,
you have to start at the bottom
and work your way up.

So, almost thirty years later,
the Acoma men
were at the bottom
of the underground mines at Ambrosia Lake,
and the Laguna men
were at the bottom of the open pit at Jackpile,
they were still training, gaining experience,
and working their way up.

And weekends, that city jail
was still full.

Ray's Story

Up at the mill
all us guys wanted to get off
the labor crew as soon as possible
so we could work as operator,
or in the sampling plant,
maybe even drive front-end loader
and such, somewhere
in mill operations.
Lacey, from Muskogee,
was one of us.
He wasn't any special person
except for one thing
which all the guys between shifts
in the changeroom showers
all gawked over
and nearly fell backwards about.
Gawd, the Okies would say,
that Indian is big,
and make remarks about his poor wife.

Well, that made Lacey noticeable
but what really made him special
was what happened.

After the guys got off the mill labor crew
usually the first place
we got put was down at the Primary Crusher,
the pit.
There, you had to stand by the vibrating chute
and watch the ore come by
from out of the bin.
Boulders and slabs of rock and dirt,
it all looked like any old hillside ground
except that mixed with it
was big steel pulleys, drill bits, timbers,
metal scrap, broken pieces of dynamite,

and cable of varying sizes.
Dangerous, no shit about that,
and you had to pick that stuff out
of the ore
before it went through the crusher
and plugged it up.

You could stop the crusher altogether
if a slab of plate steel
or something big came through,
and sometimes you had to crawl
into the crusher
and get whatever was stuck out of there,
all by hand and foot,
and hope to hell that the loader operator up top
saw the red light come on
and not load anymore ore into the bin
while you were in the crusher.
But the company
didn't like for you to stop
the crusher because
that was downtime
and the shift foreman would call down to see
what the hell was holding up production.
Well, needless to say,
nobody liked that job
and most everybody didn't stay very long
in Primary Crusher
as you got moved on up
to Secondary Crusher and so forth.
Well, except for Lacey,
he got stuck down there.

I think they said because
he couldn't read or write too well
or they didn't say anything at all.
You had to put things down
every hour by the hour
on a clipboard hung on the panel
by the Secondary Crusher

up at the end of the conveyor.
There wasn't any pencil or clipboard
down there in Primary
because all you did was pick scrap steel
and cable and pulleys from the ore
before they plugged up the company crusher
or tangled up in the conveyor rollers.

Lacey tried to get out of Primary
like most of us did,
but they just kept passing him over.
Anyway, one night—
I wasn't on that shift—
he was down there,
and I guess a mess of steel cable
came through.
Maybe he thought it was just a short length
come snaking out of the bin
because he must have grabbed it—
that's what the official report said—
and then a curl
of the heavy cable must have tangled him up
and pulled him—yeah pulled him—
right down into the jaws
of that crusher.
It makes a hell of a racket
that nobody can hear nothing
and nobody heard Lacey
if he had a chance to yell at all.

The crusher crushes
the hardest rock and don't stop
unless a solid block of steel
like a rail section comes through
and the ore just kept on crushing through
and up the conveyor
until up at Secondary
the cable fell off
and tripped the conveyor stop
and shut down operations.

Shift foreman was there at the time,
checking on production,
and he was mad as hell
because that dumb Indian
didn't catch that cable
and he rang the telephone down there.
Nobody answered of course
and the foreman started down
the long tunnel, madder now
because he must have thought Lacey
was asleep or up top talking
with the loader operator.

But on the way down, he said,
he noticed that the ore on the conveyor
was wetter than usual,
thought it was ore from 17
though it was ore from 30
running that night,
and then the next thing he noticed
was what was left of Lacey,
who he didn't recognize at all
except for the only thing
that had been noticeable about Lacey before
lying up there,
mixed in with the uranium ore from 30,
the conveyor all stopped stock still,
operations all shut down.

The conveyor all stopped stock still,
operations all shut down.

Gawd, that Indian was big,
the foreman would say,
pulling his hands apart that long,
telling his story later on,
though he didn't put that
on his report.

The company safety engineer concluded
that Lacey was negligent
in not shutting down the crusher
before he tried to get that cable
and that's why the cable got him.
The foreman said it was quite a sight by gawd,
and the guys on shift afterwards
used to wonder outloud about poor Lacey's wife.

Affirmative Action

One Fourth of July,
my kids and I went to see the parade
in Grants.
Somebody had told me that the ex-judge
had bought the old city jail,
and sure enough,
I saw that he had turned it into
a place called the Jailhouse Restaurant,
advertised as a very in place
to go in Grants.

The new and bigger city jail sat
at the edge of Martinez Park,
and the city hall walls displayed
a number of Affirmative Action signs.
I guess that could mean
that the jail was now filled
with Cajuns, Okies, Mexicans, Blacks
as well as Indians.

Crazy Gook Indians

Danny and Emmett got back from Vietnam
and went to work in the mines.
Danny said, In Section 30
one afternoon, we blasted
and my partner, Emmett, thought
we were back in Vietnam,
back in the tunnels,
after the enemy, you know.
He picked up that drill
like it was an M-60
and tried to defend us against
the shift boss who'd been in the Marines too.
I got Emmett quieted down
and held him in my arms for a while.
The boss just laughed
and later on I heard him laughing
with the superintendent
about the crazy gook Indians
on his shift.
I guess I should have let my partner
defend us against that Marine.

Out to Tsaile Lake

By the lakeside,
there was a woman and a man.

I asked them how many fish they'd caught.
We just got here, the man said.

A little white dog snarled and barked at me.
The woman stuck her fishing rod at the dog
and called, Amy, Amy, pipe down,
it's alright, it's just an Indian.

I asked them where they were from.
We just got here, the man said again.

Out of the clear blue sky,
the man said, Coming up the road
from Grants we saw a turrible wreck.
Guess it was maybe some Indians.
They was kinda scattered around
and no ambulance in sight.

The little dog kept snarling at me.

The woman stuck her fishing rod at the man
and said, He said to me this morning,
Let's go out to Tsaile Lake,
Indian fish are maybe hungry.

The little white dog kept on snarling.
Amy, Amy, calm down, don't fret yourself.

Around a bend of the lake,
a Navajo man was fishing too.
I told him I was from Acoma.
He said he was from Shiprock.
He said, I work ten years in the mines.
Underground, in Colorado.
I work at Ambrosia Lake too, underground.
It's too wet. I'm not no gopher,
I'm a dry Navajo. He laughed. Underground.
So I quit that and now I'm looking.

Maybe I have to go back to Colorado.
Underground. He said, At Ambrosia Lake,
I work with big Acoma guy name Concho.
I got my dog, pointing
to a huge St. Bernard pulling a chain,
at Milan's in Gallup.

Mexican guy need cash and I got it.
Because he's a big one,
I call my dog Concho
for big Acoma miner.
Laughing, I said, When I see Concho
I'll tell him there's a big dog
named for him in Navajo country.

Yeah, the Navajo man said,
I hope I get a job pretty soon.
It cost too much to live with no money.
I went to Albuquerque to buy a truck.
I almost have it at Galles Chevy
but they call BIA in Window Rock
and they said I have to give them
five hundred dollars more
before they give it to me.
Dammit, I already have one thousand
in cash from selling my cows
and if they didn't want it, forget it.
I said, Hell with it,
you don't want my money I'll keep it.
Man can't get credit these days
for being alive. Laughing,
I laughed with him. He said,
Maybe I have better luck with fish.

The First Hard Core

Herb, me, Art, and Wiley
rode car pool together for a while.
Herb was from Houston
and most of his life since teenage,
he worked on the docks

and the oil rigs on the Gulf.
He was quite a talker.
One time he said—Oh Herb said
a lot of things but I remember this—
Hey chief, how come
you all out here don't have names
like regular Indians supposed to.
Simon. Art. Martinez. Wiley.
But Wiley is Okie too
so I guess that figures for him.
But I mean names like Straight Arrow,
Running Bear, Broken Bow, Sitting Bull,
stuff like that. Goldwater.
Goldwater? He ain't no Indian,
must be a Jew trick or something.
How come, chief, how come, huh?

I was just a teenager
when I went to work in the mills and mines,
and I didn't know how to answer him
so he'd believe me if he could.
I just said, I don't know.

Herb used to have an observation
which was the same as a rule
for him too I think.
We white people got our niggers
to look down on.
Mexicans here got you Indians
to look down on.
And you all got Navajos
to look down on,
but who the hell Navajos
got to look down on?

I couldn't figure out how to answer
that one either if it was a question at all.
I guess I wanted to tell him
we were working on land stolen from Acoma
and that Martinez was a Navajo man
on whose land was discovered uranium

which gave us our jobs.
But I just said, I don't know.

That was when it was an election year.
Herb said, Who you gonna vote for,
chief? Kennedy?
Don't be fooled now.
Remember, just like Goldwater is a Jew
even if his name sounds Indian,
Kennedy is a rich commie sympathizer.
Who you voting for, chief?

I was just a kid then as I said,
and I learned a lot from him actually
because Herb was the first hard core
I ever met personally.
But I didn't know how to answer him then.
I just felt powerless to answer.
I just said I didn't know.

To Change in a Good Way

Bill and Ida
lived in the mobile home park
west of Milan.
They'd come out with Kerr-McGee
when the company first started
sinking shafts at Ambrosia Lake.
That would be in '58 or '59.
He was an electricians helper
and Ida was a housewife
though for a while she worked
over at that 24-hour Catch-All store.
But mostly she liked to be around home,
the trailer park, and tried to plant

a little garden on the little patch
of clay land that came with the mobile home.
She missed Oklahoma
like Bill did too who always said
they were going to just stay long enough
to get a down payment, save enough,
for some acreage in eastern Oklahoma.

That's what he told Pete,
the Laguna man he came to be friends with
at Section 17.
Pete worked as a skip tender
and once in a while they worked
the same shift and rode car pool together.

You're lucky you got some land, Pete,
Bill would say.
It's not much but it's some land,
Pete would agree.

He and Mary, his wife, had a small garden
which they'd plant in the spring.
Chili, couple rows of sweetcorn, squash,
beans, even had lettuce, cucumbers,
and radishes, onions.
They irrigated from the small stream,
the Rio de San Jose, which runs through
Acoma and Laguna land.
Ida just had the clay red ground
which she had planted that first spring
they'd spent in New Mexico with lettuce
and radishes and corn, but the only thing
that ever really came up was the corn
and it was kind of stunted and wilty looking.
She watered the little patch
from the little green plastic hose
hooked up to the town water system
that started running dry about mid-June.

One Saturday, Pete and Mary
and Bill and Ida
were all shopping at the same time

at the Sturgis Food Mart in Milan,
and the women became friends too.
They all went over to the mobile home park
and sat around and drank pepsis and talked.
Ida and Bill didn't have any kids
but Mary and Pete had three.

They're at home,
staying out of trouble I hope, Mary said.
Bill had a younger brother nicknamed Slick.
He had a photo of him
sitting on the TV stand shelf.
Bill was proud of his little brother.
He was in the Army.
Bill said, In Vietnam.
I worry about him some
but at least he's learnt a trade.
He's a Spec-4 in Signal.
Slick's been kind of wild,
so I know about trouble.
Bill passed Slick's photo
to Pete and Mary.

Ida took Mary outside
to show her her garden.
It's kinda hard trying to grow anything
here, Ida said, different from Oklahoma.
Mary said, I think you need something
in it, Ida, to break up the packed clay.
Maybe some sheep stuff.
I'll tell Pete to bring you some.

The next weekend Pete brought some sheep stuff
and spread it around the wilty plants.
Work it around and into the ground,
he said, but it'll be till next year
that it will be better.
He brought another pickup load later on.

Ida and Bill went down to Laguna too,
to the reservation,

and they met Pete and Mary's kids.
Ida admired their small garden.
Slick was visiting
on leave and he came with them.
He had re-upped, had a new Spec-5 patch
on his shoulder and had bought a motorcycle.
He was on his way to another tour.
Bill said, I wish he hadn't done that.
Folks at home are worried too.
Good thing your boys aren't old enough.

In the yard, the kids, including Slick,
were playing catch with a softball.
He wasn't much older than Pete's
and Mary's oldest.
Slick had bright and playful eyes,
handsome, and Bill was right
to be proud of his kid brother.
I'm gonna make sure
that young jackoff goes to college
after the damn Army, Bill said.

After that, they'd visit each other.
Ida would come help Mary with her garden.
A couple times, the kids
went to stay with Ida
when Bill worked graveyard or swing
because she didn't like to be alone.
The kids liked that too,
staying in town or what there was
of it at the edge of Milan
at the mobile home amidst others
sitting on the clay hard ground.
The clay had come around to being workable
with the sheep stuff in it.
Ida planted radishes and lettuce
and carrots and corn,
even tomatoes and chili,
and she was so proud of her growing plants
that summer.

One afternoon, up at Section 17,
Bill got a message from the foreman
to call Ida.
They were underground replacing wire
and he had to take the skip up.
He called from the payphone
outside the mine office.
Pete held the skip for him
and when he came back Bill said,
I gotta get my lunchpail
and go home.

Something wrong, Bill? Pete asked.
You okay?
Yeah, Bill said, something happened
to Slick, the folks called from Claremore.
Hope it's not serious, Pete said.

On the way home after shift,
Pete stopped at Bill's and Ida's.
Ida answered the door and showed him in.
Bill was sitting on the couch.
He had a fifth of Heaven Hill halfway empty.
Pete, Bill said, Slick's gone.
No more Slick. Got killed by stepping
on a mine, an American mine—
isn't that the shits, Pete?
Dammit Pete, just look at that kid.
He pointed at the photo on the TV stand.
Pete didn't say anything at first
and then he said, Aamoo o dyumuu,
and put his arm around Bill's shoulders.
Bill poured him some Heaven Hill
and Ida told him they were leaving
for Claremore next morning as soon as
they could pack and the bank opened.
Should get there by evening, she said.
And then Pete left.

When Pete got home, he told Mary
what had happened.

She said, Tomorrow morning
on your way to work, drop me off there.
I want to see Ida.
Pete said, You can go ahead
and drive me to work and take the truck.

That night they sat at the kitchen table
with the kids and tied feathers
and scraped willow sticks
and closed them in a cornhusk
with cotton, beads, and tobacco.
The next morning, Mary and Pete went by
the mobile home park.
Bill and Ida were loading the last
of their luggage into their car.
After greetings and solaces,
Mary said, We brought you some things.
She gave Ida a loaf of Laguna bread.
For your lunch, she said,
and Ida put it in the ice chest.
Pete took a white corn ear
and the cornhusk bundle
out of a paper bag he carried,
and he showed them to Bill.
He said, This is just a corn, Bill,
Indian corn. The People call it Kasheshi.
Just corn. You take it with you,
or you can keep it here.
You can plant it.
It's to know that life will keep on,
your life will keep on.
Just like Slick will be planted again.
He'll be like that, like seed planted,
like corn seed, the Indian corn.
But you and Ida, your life
will grow on.

He put the corn ear back into the bag
and then he held out the husk bundle.
He said, I guess I don't remember
some of what is done, Bill,

Indian words, songs for it,
what it all is, even how this is made
just a certain way but I know
that it is important to do this.
You take this too, but you don't keep it.
It's for Slick, for his travel
from this life among us
to another place of being.
You and Ida are not Indian,
but it doesn't make any difference.
It's for all of us, this kind of way,
with corn and this, Bill.
You take these sticks and feathers
and you put them somewhere you think
you should, someplace important
that you think might be good, maybe
to change life in a good way,
that you think Slick
would be helping us with.
And you say a few things
about it to him when you do.
You take it now, and I know
it may not sound easy to do
but don't worry yourself too much.
Slick's okay now, he'll be helping us,
and you'll be fine too.

Pete put the paper bag in Bill's hand,
and they all shook hands and hugged
and Mary drove Pete on to work.

After they left, Bill went inside
their trailer home and took out the corn.
He looked at it for a while,
thinking, Just corn, just Indian corn,
just your life to go on, Ida and you.
And then he put the corn by the photo,
by Slick on the TV stand.
And then he wondered about the husk bundle.
He couldn't figure it out.
He'd grown up in Claremore all his life,

Indians living all around him,
folks and some teachers said so,
Cherokees in the Ozark hills, Creeks
over to Muskogee, but Mary and Pete
were the first Indians he'd ever known.
He held the bundle in his hand,
thinking, and then he decided not to take it
to Oklahoma, and put it in the cupboard.
They locked up their trailer and left.

Bill and Ida returned a week later.
Most of the folks had been at the funeral,
and everything had gone alright.
The folks were upset a whole lot,
but there wasn't much else to do
except comfort them.
Some of the other folks said
that someone had to make the sacrifice
for freedom of democracy and all that,
and that's what Slick had died of, for.
He's done his duty for America,
look at how much the past folks
had to put up with, living a hard life,
fighting off Indians to build homes
on new land so we could live the way
we are right now, advanced and safe
from peril like the Tuls' Tribune
said the other day Sunday that's what
Slick died for, just like past folks.
That's what a couple relatives
advised about and Bill tried to say
what was bothering him, that the mine
that Slick had stepped on was American
and that the fact he was in a dangerous place
was because he was in an Army
that was American, and it didn't seem
to be the same thing as what they were saying
about past folks fighting
Indians for democracy
and it didn't seem right somehow.

But nobody really heard him,
they just asked him about his job
with Kerr-McGee, told him the company
had built itself another building in Tulsa,
Kerr's gonna screw those folks in New Mexico
just like he has folks here being Senator.
Ida and Bill visited for a while,
comforted his folks for a while,
and then they left for Milan.

By the time they got back to their mobile home,
Bill knew what he was going to do
with the bundle of sticks and feathers.
He'd been thinking about it all the way
on I-40 from Oklahoma City, running
it through his mind, what Slick had died of.
Well because of the bomb, stepping
on the wrong place, being in
a dangerous place, but something else.
The reason was something else, and though
Bill wasn't completely sure about it yet
he felt he was beginning to know.
And he knew what he was going to do
with the bundle in the cupboard.

The next morning, he put it in his lunchpail
and went to work, reporting
to the mine office first.
He changed into his work clothes
and put on his yellow slicker because
they were going down that morning,
and he was glad for that for once.
He took the paper bag out of his pail
and put it in his overall pocket.
After they went down he said
he was going to go and check
some cable and he made his way to a far end
of a stope that had been mined out
and stopped and put the bundle down
behind a slab of rock.

He didn't know what to do next,
and then he thought of what Pete said.
Say something about it. Well, he thought,
I guess, Slick, you was a good boy,
kind of wild, but good. I got this here
Indian thing, feathers and sticks,
and at home, at home we got the corn
by your picture, and Pete and Mary said
to do this because it's important
even if we're Okies
and not Indians who do this.
It's for your travel they said
and to help us with our life here
from where you are at now and they said
to maybe change things in a good way
for a good life and God knows us Okies
always wanted that though we maybe
have been wrong sometimes.
Well, I'm gonna leave this here
by the rock. Pete said he didn't know
exactly the right thing
but somehow I believe he's more righter
than we've ever been, and now I'm trying too.
So you help us now, Slick.

We need it, all the help we can get,
even if it's just so much as holding up
the roof of this mine that the damn company
don't put enough timbers and bolts in, Bill said.
And then he stepped back and left.

When he got home that evening,
he told Ida what he had done, and she said,
Next spring I'm gonna plant that Indian corn,
and Slick, if he's gonna help hold up
the roof of Section 17, better be able
to help with breaking up that clay dirt too.
Bill smiled and then chuckled with Ida.

Final Solution: Jobs, Leaving

They would leave
on Sundays from the depot in Grants.
It seemed always, always, so final.
Goodbye. Goodbye Daddy. Daddy,
please come back. Please don't go.
Daddy. But they would leave.

Winslow.
        Flagstaff.
                Seligman.
Barstow.

We had to buy groceries,
had to have clothes, homes, roofs,
windows. Surrounded by the United States,
we had come to need money.

The solution was to change,
to leave, to go to jobs.

                Utah.
California.
       Idaho.
        Oregon.

The children would cry.
The women would be so angry.
So angry.
Silent, we left.
We didn't want to leave, but
we left.

"I don't want you and your brothers
to ever have to work for the railroad."
They kept the railroad repaired,
and the trains raced through
their land. Hearts. Blood. Bones
and skin. Wrenched muscles.

"You ever pick up a rail?
With your bare hands." Your sweat
burning in your eyes. Blood. Heart.
Skin. Bones. And they died too.
"I hope." How much they hated,
how much they hoped. How much.

American Fork, Utah, February, 1959.
Dear Mama & Children,
I hope you are all well
as I am. Children, help your mother
and take care of each others
and around our home. Remember
that you must always love
your mothers. Think of the prayers
for the land. Mama, I wish
I was home with all of you.
I will be home in a few weeks.
I love you all. Make sure
you feed the horses. My love
and hugs to each of you and Mama,
                    Daddy.

Saw him in Seligman.
Or was it Valentine. Or Phoenix.
Or somewhere. "He step off
the train. That was the last time
I saw him. My friend." Tears.
Wine doesn't work. They died too.

One week, two weeks, three weeks,
months, we waited. Years.
Train. O Daddy, O Daddy. Train
would come thundering, thundering
thundering toward us. Hearts.
Blood. Bones and skin. Love
and hope. O Daddy. Please train.

The children would laugh or cry
or be so silent.
The women were so angry.

Yes, we would wait again. Weeks, weeks, months, but not those years again. O Daddy, never those years. Never again those years. Our own solution will be strength: hearts, blood, bones, skin, hope and love. The woman anger and courage risen as the People's voice again.

Stuff: Chickens and Bombs

Wiley, from Arkansas,
and I worked a couple times
in Yellowcake.

Wiley usually worked in scrap yard,
sorting scrap so the company
could sell it or use it again.
I usually worked in Crushing
where the uranium stuff
was just rocks and dirt.

In Yellowcake,
we packed the processed stuff
which is a yellow powder
into fifty-five gallon drums
and wheeled them out
to waiting trucks
bound for where we didn't know.

Once,
thinking I knew something,
I told Wiley
that the government used
the yellowcake for bombs
and reactors and experiments.

Wiley studied my face a minute,
then he spat on the ground
and said, "Once, I worked

in a chicken factory.
We plucked and processed chickens
so people could eat 'em.
I don't know what the hell else
you could do with them."

That's the Place Indians Talk About

At a meeting in California I was talking with an elder Paiute man.
    He had been a rangerider and a migrant laborer. He spoke about
    Coso Hot Springs, a sacred and healing place for the Shoshonean
    peoples, enclosed within the China Lake Naval Station. Like Los
    Alamos Scientific Laboratories in New Mexico, the naval station
    is a center for the development, experimentation, and testing of
    U.S. military weapons. The elder man, wearing thick glasses and
    a cowboy hat, said, "That's the place Indians talk about."

We go up there and camp.
Several days, we stay there.
We have to take horses, wagons,
or walk.
And we would stay
for the days we have to.

The Coso Hot Springs would talk to us.
And we would talk to it.
The People have to talk to it.
That's the place Indians talk about.
That's the place.

Children, women, men,
we would all go up there.
You drink that water, it makes you well.
You put it on your hands, face, all over,
and you get well, all well.

That's the place Indians talk about,
the Coso Hot Springs the People go to.

You take a flint like this,
a hard stone in your hand,
and you give it like this.
When you pray.
When you sing.
When you talk to the hot springs.
You talk with it when it talks to you.

Something from there,
from down in there is talking to you.
You could hear it.
You listen.

      Listen.
You can hear it.
The stones in the earth rattling together.

The stones down there moving around each other.
When we pray.
When we sing.
When we talk with the stones
rattling in the ground
and the stones moving in the ground.
That's the place Indians talk about.

Oh,
we stay there for some days.
You could hear it talking.
From far,
from far away inside, the moving power.
From far away, coming to us,
coming to us pretty soon.
Getting closer, getting close,
the power is getting close,
and the ground is hot and shaking.

Something is doing that
and the People know that.
They have to keep talking.
Praying, that's the Indian way.

Singing, that's the Indian way.
And pretty soon, it's there.
You know it's all around.
It's right there,
and the People are right there.
That's the place Indians talk about.

And now,
they have a fence around the Coso Hot Springs.
We go up there, but they have a fence around.
They have a government fence all around Coso Hot Springs.
Since World War II, the Navy of the government
has a fence around that place.
The People go up there to talk with the hot springs,
to use the power, to keep ourselves well with,
but there is a fence with locks all around,
and we have to talk with the Navy people
so they can let us inside the fence to the hot springs.

We go up there to talk with the hot springs power
but the Navy tells us we have to talk to them.
We don't like it, to have to do that.
We don't want to talk to the government fence,
the government Navy.
That's the place the Indian people are talking about now.

For many years,
the People went up there.
Families from all over.
From Nevada, from Utah, from Arizona,
from north California, from south,
from all over, from anyplace.
Families have to travel by horses,
wagons, and now by cars, and walking.
We keep going up there,
for all this many years, we have to.
To keep talking to the power
of the power in the earth, we have to.
That's the Indian way.

We don't like to talk to the fence and the Navy
but for a while we will and pretty soon

we will talk to the hot springs power again.
That's the place Indians talk about.

Listen,
that's the way you hear.
Pretty soon, you can hear it,
coming far away
deep in the ground, deep down there coming,
the voice of the power coming,
closer and closer.
Listen, that's the way you hear it.
From the earth,
the moving power of the voice
and the People talking.
Praying, you know, singing soft too.

Hearing,
that's the way you listen.
The People talking,
telling the power to come to them
and pretty soon it will come.
It will come,
the moving power of the voice,
the moving power of the earth,
the moving power of the People.
That's the place Indian People talk about.

We Have Been Told Many Things but We Know This to Be True

The land. The people.
They are in relation to each other.
We are in a family with each other.
The land has worked with us.
And the people have worked with it.

This is true:
               Working for the land
and the people—it means life
and its continuity.
Working not just for the people,
but for the land too.
We are not alone in our life;
we cannot expect to be.
The land has given us our life,
and we must give life back to it.

The land has worked for us
to give us life—
breathe and drink and eat from it
gratefully—
and we must work for it
to give it life.
Within this relation of family,
it is possible to generate life.
This is the work involved.
Work is creative then.
It is what makes for reliance,
relying upon the relation of land and people.
The people and the land are reliant
upon each other.
This is the kind of self-reliance
that has been—
before the liars, thieves, and killers—
and this is what we must continue
to work for.
By working in this manner,
for the sake of the land and people
to be in vital relation
with each other,
we will have life,
and it will continue.

We have been told many things,
but we know this to be true:
the land and the people.

What I Mean

Agee. I don't mean that Agee,
I mean Agee from home.
He was just one of us, but a hero.
I mean not in a big way but real,
because he was one of us.

He was a young guy
who never got beyond nineteen.
We were the same age though in school
he was always behind
and the teachers were always on him
for not doing well.
Agee was always laughing and fooling around
and talking Indian
(you couldn't do that)
and making English sound like Indian
(you couldn't do that either.)
English had to be English,
that was the real American way,
and Indian was just Indian—
the teachers so much as said that to us.

Agee quit school in junior high
and went to work in the mines.
He went to work because his family was poor
like all our families were poor.
He was one of the first guys from home
in the mines and probably the youngest.
After high school when I started working
for Kermac mill at Ambrosia Lake,
he was at Haystack working underground.

You know it's funny—
I mean this: teachers in school
were always on him
because he couldn't read
(or wouldn't)

or couldn't talk English
(or wouldn't)
but once when I was in Grandma's Cafe
in Milan where the guys I rode with
sometimes stopped to pick up bag lunches,
I was surprised.
Grandma's was usually crowded
with miners and millworkers
but not many of us Indians
ever went in there, and Agee was there.
And he was talking. I mean talking.

That may not sound like a big deal,
but this is what I mean:
We didn't talk much.
Some people say Indians are just like that,
shy and reserved and polite,
but that's mostly crap. Lots of times
we were just plain scared
and we kept our mouths shut.
I mean Grants and Milan and the mines
between Haystack and Ambrosia Lake,
all that area used to be Indian land—
Acoma land—but it was surveyed
by the government and stolen
at the turn of the century
and there was plenty to say
but we didn't say it.
I mean being Indian wasn't the safest
thing to be in town
so we didn't say much, much less
be in Grandma's Cafe arguing
with white miners who made jokes
about squaws and called you chief.
I mean Agee was talking.

And he was reading too,
from the union contract
which was the issue of the argument.
That was right before the strike in 1961.
Most of us few Indian workers

didn't know much
about the mine unions and Agee
was one of the first members from home
and he was arguing for the strike.
As I said before, most of us
didn't say much of anything.
We were just glad for the jobs we had,
union or no union, but Agee,
when the workers went out on strike later,
spoke for us saying that Indians
were just like other workers
and he wasn't shy or reserved
saying that in English that sounded
Okie and Mexican and Indian.

Later on,
Agee went down to Silver City
when the workers went on strike there.
He was always doing that,
helping folks, especially old folks,
and it didn't matter who.
Well, down there, one night,
he was changing a tire
or pushing a stalled car or something,
he was struck accidentally—
that's what they told folks at home,
and maybe it was. And maybe too
it was because Agee was
just another worker,
just another Indian,
there was nothing else necessary
for them to tell us.

But what I mean is:
Although Agee never made it beyond young,
the mines were still there
and the workers were still fighting
and old people still needed help
and the language of our struggle
just sounds and reads like an Indian,

Okie, Cajun, Black, Mexican hero story—
that's what we mean.
That's what we mean.

Mama's and Daddy's Words

Duwah hahtse dzah.
This is the land.
It is our life, your life,
my life, life.
Hahtse. Naya. Kutra tsahtee.
Land. Mother. Your breath, living.

You young people
you have a chance.
I've worked in the sawmills,
road gang, fencing, picking crops,
herding sheep, on the railroad.
Sure it was hard,
hot sun, your back breaking
hands all torn, low pay.
Sure it was hard
to put up with them,
with names they called you,
sure it's hard.
But you have to fight
by working.
You have to fight
by working for the land and the People,
to show them,
to work for the People and the land.
Emii i Hanoh.
Amoo o Hanoh.
Compassion for all the People.

Love for all the People.
Emii i amoo o Hanoh eh hahtse.
Sure it's hard,
sure it's not easy
working for the People and the land,
to fight for the People and the land.
That's the only way that they'll learn.
That's the only way.

Returning It Back, You Will Go On

Corporate power companies
from the East and from the West
bought the processed uranium
from the corporate oil and mining companies
who mined the land.
That's Indian land.
Crownpoint. Smith Lake, Haystack,
Church Rock, San Mateo, Ambrosia Lake,
Laguna, Seboyeta. For sure, those names
don't sound like Indian names,
but for sure those are Indian lands
and the People who live there
are Indian People.
Hanoh stu tah ah.
We are Hanoh. People. Hanoh. People.

Power companies and corporations,
railroads, agribusiness, electronics,
states, cities, towns,
the men and women who work in them,
all of them—all of America—

take and takes from the land and People.
The land lets you.
Kudrawaa yah ahni.
The People let you.
Kudrawaa yah ahni.
But America must give back.
That is the only way the land will regenerate.
That is the only way the People will be freed.

When you plant something,
watch it grow, nourish it,
so carefully, so gently, sing, talk,
watch it grow, harvest it,
prepare it, pray, speak about it
to others, remind them, watch your children grow,
use and eat it and return it back.
With great care and planning,
with compassion and love,
you will grow, you will go on,
and you will plant again
and the plant will grow.
Returning it back, returning
it back, you will go on, life will go on.
That's what the People say.
That's what the land says.

If we don't do that,
life will continue to be exploited,
the land will be used up
and the People will remain colonized and powerless,
and the city jail
will still be full of Indians.
                              Until soon,
the jail will not be enough
to hold all the nations of the People,
and they will have risen.
They will have risen.

This Song: Beating The Heartbeat

Before my father returned
to the continuing earth life,
before he traveled back north,
we sat with him for long hours.
Early, early one morning
at the hospital, just he and I
and the oscilloscope above his bed,
beating the heartbeat of his life,
beating the heartbeat of my life,
were together.
This song remembers him:

Heart beating
Heart beating
Heart beating
        beating
           beating
              beating
                  beating
beating beating.

Heart beating
Heart beating
Heart beating
        beating
           beating
              beating
                  beating
beating beating.

Life beating
Earth beating

All beating
       beating
           beating
              beating
                 beating
beating beating.

Life beating
Earth beating
All beating
       beating
           beating
              beating
                 beating
beating beating.

Heart beating
Life beating
We shall know
       living
           living
              living
                 living
living living.

Heart beating
Life beating
We shall know
       living
           living
              living
                 living
living living.

We shall know living.
We shall know living.

It Will Come; It Will Come

Haitah muumuu ka
Haitah muumuu ka
Haitah muumuu muumuu muumuu muumuu ka.

Where from is it thundering.
Thundering, the People working.
Thundering, the People's voices.
Thundering, the movement of the struggle.
Thundering, the power of the Land.
Thundering, the coming Rain.
It will come, it will come.
With compassion.
With courage.
With unity.
With understanding.
With love.
We shall endure.
We shall go on.
We shall have victory.
We shall know living.
We shall know living.

II   NO MORE SACRIFICES

Our Homeland, A National Sacrifice Area

It was only the second day,
and I was on my way home
from being with Srhakaiya.
It is the mountain west
of Aacqu.
    I was sick,
feeling a sense of "otherness."
How can I describe it?
An electric current
coursing in ghost waves through me?
    "Otherness."

I was raised in McCartys which is one of the small villages in the
Acoma community. The people say Aacqu. Aacqumeh hanoh, we call
ourselves. New Mexico and U.S. maps say Acoma, The Sky City.

McCartys is right off Interstate 40, the old U.S. 66, sixty-five miles
west of Albuquerque, the largest city in New Mexico. McCarty was
the name of an Irishman who operated the water pumps which sucked
water from the nearby chuna, the Rio de San Jose. The farming Aac-
qumeh community where the pumps were located on the AT&SF rail-
road became known as McCartys Stop.

U.S. and New Mexico maps and tourist bureaus do not know the
Aacqumeh hanoh's name for the local community. It is Deetseya-
mah—The North Door. Looking northward from Aacqu and the tall
rock monolith on which the mother pueblo sits, there is an opening,

337

like a gateway, between two mesas. Looking northward, too, from Aacqu, one can see Kaweshtima—Snowed Peaked—a dark blue misted mother mountain. Those Aacqumeh names do not appear anywhere except in the people's hearts and souls and history and oral tradition, and in their love. But you will find the easy labels: Mt. Taylor, Elevation 11,950 ft., and Acoma: The Sky City.

"Otherness."
I can't describe it
and perhaps there is such a sensation.
I had drunk some water the evening before
on the northside of Srhakaiya.
The spring was scummed over.
A Garden Deluxe wine empty lay nearby.

Years ago, in the 1950's,
when I was a boy of 9 or 10,
I'd come with my father
and the sheep we herded.
The sheep drank at a cistern,
and we drank from the spring.
The clear cold water was covered
with heavy plank boards
and the pool was fed by the seep
from the shale rock.
The pool had a stone lining.

Aacqumeh hanoh came to their valley from a direction spoken of as the northwest. The place they came to had been prepared for them, and the name, Aacqu, therefore means that: Which Is Prepared. When they arrived in the flat valley sheltered by red and orange cliffs, they knew they had found what had been prepared by their leaders and instructions from earlier generations of the people.

The valley of Aacqu is a beautiful and peaceful place. It must have been wealthy with grass growing in the dark fertile soil nourished by the nearby volcanic mountain slopes and a number of perennial springs gushing forth. It must have been cool and restful in the shade of the tall mesa which would be their eventual home. Their journey had been long and difficult from the northwest through vast experience, trials, and crises. Kaashkatruti, that's where we lived before, the people say in their oral tradition, pointing northwestward.

338

Pueblo Bonito in Chaco Canyon
is maintained by the U.S. Park Service.
Northwards, 65 miles away,
is Aztec National Monument.
To the northwest, another 85 miles,
is Mesa Verde National Park.
The park service has guided tours,
printed brochures, clean rest rooms,
and the staff is friendly, polite,
and very helpful.
You couldn't find a better example
of Americanhood anywhere.
The monuments, or ruins
as they are called, are very well kept
by the latest technology
in preserving antiquity.

At Mesa Verde, not long ago,
they had Esther in a glass case.
She was a child, born
from a woman, 1000 years ago.
The U.S. Park Service
was reluctant to let her go
when some Indian people
demanded her freedom.
Government bureaucrats
said Indians were insensitive
to U.S. heritage.
For years, they sold
postcards of Esther.
Maybe they still do.
By pushing buttons, thousands
of yearly tourists to these places
can get an audio-taped narration.

See Museum For More Information.

Ghoomi is now the main springs in the valley. Water flows in no
large amount from deep shale and gathers in steel troughs installed
some years ago. The overflow runs into a small earthen dam.

The elders of the Aacqumeh hanoh speak about the numbers of springs in the valley. In olden times. Now there are several minor wells pumped by windmills; water barely trickles into steel holding tanks and troughs. By July there is only dust in the bottoms. Ghoomi has never been known to run dry, but it is watched anxiously. The old and young people go by the springs frequently because the water from it is sweet and cold.

The water in the cistern
on the northside of Srhakaiya
was not mountain cold.
It smelled
and tasted sour.
But I was thirsty,
and I drank.

Ghoomi and the windmill on the mesa above it and the Gahnippa springs are in a line which runs from Aacqu to the northwest. The line runs over mesas with juniper and sparse grass; it crosses arroyos filled with sand except when it rains in August. Above Deetseyamah are volcanic cliffs, the dark sharp edges of a massive mesa extending southward from the slopes of Kaweshtima. On the mesa is another windmill, and on the northwestern slope is Lobo Canyon and the springs there. Perhaps it's true as I've heard: these springs are in a direct line with each other, and they have never run dry. And on the northwesterly line is Ambrosia Lake, forty miles from Aacqu.

After I drank
I ate.
    Afterwards,
listened to the wind
sweeping across the cliffs,
weaving in the pines.
Ten miles to the north
is the Rio de San Jose.
Alongside is the AT&SFRY.
Heard a freight train wail.
As August dark night
Summer fell,

I was cold and alone.
The lights of Grants,
the Uranium Capital of the World
splashed and shimmered
to the west.

Srhakaiya and, south of it, Dinnibhuu, an uplift west of Aacqu are
volcanic masses originating from the epoch when Kaweshtima was an
active volcano. Their soils have washed unto the flat valley around
Aacqu. In the summertime, usually in late July and August, the people
can see silvery water entering eastward out of the canyons from the
mountains into the corn, pumpkin, and bean fields they have planted.

When I was a boy, we had fields in the valley near some white sand-
stone cliffs. I loved to run barefoot in the cool early Summer soil as my
father plowed behind our horses, Charley and Bill. My mother and I
would walk behind and drop corn seeds spaced a footstep apart. We
scattered pumpkin seeds and melon seeds and covered them with a
thin layer of the soft sandy soil. Friends and I played games, hunted,
and explored the cliffs and among the huge boulders above our fields.
In the evenings when we were called to supper, we would race to our
farming camps.

When the Spaniard came in 1540, he found Aacqu very wealthy in
its material security, social well-being, and spiritual integrity. The
people were clothed in cotton fabrics and handsomely dressed animal
skins. The streets of the city, as he called it, were very clean and or-
derly, and he was impressed by its location on a magnificent rock. In
fact, he called Aacqu by such terms as his European knowledge knew:
majestic and regal. The Aacqumeh hanoh welcomed him, fed him, and
gave him many gifts. His men, eager and hungry, were struck by the
comely features and physique of the men, children, and women. The
Spaniard, courtly and militaristic, could not help but note in his jour-
nals the ceremonious manner in which he and his men were attended.
They must have felt like kings, even godlike, instead of the mercenaries,
errand boys, and mystics that they were. Although the Spaniard re-
ported to his superiors in Mexico and Spain some qualms about the
harsh land in New Spain and a notable reserve in the people, he recom-
mended occupation and settlement because of the natural material
wealth of the land and the generosity and cooperative nature of the
people. There was no visible gold or jewels or treasure as had been

fabled, but the land and people were obviously productive and the potential for colonization and profit was worthy of royal and private investment. The Spaniard was impressed indeed.

Grants is a small town
in western Cibola County.
There was a logging industry
in the 1920's and 30's.
In the latter 40's to the mid 50's
it hailed itself as the Carrot Capital
of the World, no less.
The last vestige of a lumber industry
was a box factory in 1960.
There is a small gypsum mine
above Lobo Canyon
and a crushing plant in town.
    In the night I heard
the wail of the train again.
    I thought about McCarty,
the Irishman.

Other than the flood-plain fields in the valley surrounding Aacqu, the Aacqumeh hanoh have irrigated fields in the Rio de San Jose valley twelve miles north. Early Spanish colonists found small farming communities there. They noted the irrigation system, as they did also that along the Rio Grande to the east, and they compared their design and technology to those in Mexico. The river was fed out of the lava beds to the west from the Zuni Mountains, from the north by Kaweshtima, and from the present Ambrosia Lake area to the northwest.

The water ran sparkling clear, abundant, and fast, and the people irrigated their food plants and drank from it. In the oral tradition of storytelling the chuna swirls and is vigorous and healthy. But since the time of the railroads, the logging town, the carrot fields, and the construction of Bluewater Dam in the 1930's, the people have watched the river. Very anxiously, the people kept going to Ghoomi and Gahnippa springs, and they thought about the northwest direction toward Ambrosia Lake. There seemed to be enough water during the working years of the Irishman and his pumps, but now there was hardly enough for the people who wanted to and could farm.

The railroads were the first large industrial users of the water be-
longing to the land and people. They found it easy enough to get; they
simply took it. The railroads had been given grants of land by the U.S.
government and they got right of way through Indian land. Choice
Aacqumeh lands which were the flatlands along the Rio de San Jose
were taken as rights of way. To the east, the farm lands of Laguna and
Isleta were the right of way as were those of the people's on the Rio
Grande to the northeast. As it pushed westward, the railroads took
right of way through Navajo people's land too. As it was easy enough
to take water from the land and feed the train engines, it was easy
enough to disregard the farming livelihood that was taken away. The
railroads replaced the traditional agricultural livelihood with wage
labor which maintained the railroads—thereafter the people would
make their living by working for the railroad, just like the Irishman.

Our family hauled water
in fifty-gallon drums
for use as drinking water.
My father built a sled
on which we'd put the barrels.
Over the barrels we stretched tarp
as a cover.
My mother said the people
drank
from the nearby river
when she was a girl.
But when I was a boy,
we used it only for washing clothes.
We could not drink it.

Grants took its name from a lumber mill, and it grew into a settle-
ment when the railroad was built. Logs and lumber were shipped from
there. Livestock, including cattle and sheep raised by Aacqumeh,
Laguna, and Navajo people, were a local business activity. Actually, the
village of San Rafael south of the present city of Grants was the origi-
nal settlement. It was an outpost for mercantile interests and a mili-
tary base of operations in the war of extermination against the Navajo
people. Later, Grants became a trade center though not as large as
Gallup seventy miles westward.

After Bluewater Dam was built, the valley below it settled by
Mormon families became truck farms with the main crop being
carrots. Grants called itself The Carrot Capital of the World. In the
early 50's, it was a town of 5,000. The Bluewater fields were worked
seasonally by Acoma, Laguna, Navajo, and Indo-Hispanic laborers.
Most of the work was stoop labor in the fields and in packing sheds.
By the mid 50's, Grants did not boast anymore than a railroad depot,
a bank, several general merchandise and food stores, a theater, post
office, a grade school and high school, a jail, and several churches and
bars. There were a few modestly wealthy families whose origin was
in the mercantile-trading post business which had supplied railroad
contractors and the military. To the east were San Fidel, Cubero, and
Seboyeta, which were Indo-Hispanic settlements which were as poor
as the Laguna and Acoma communities.

The poor are as permanent as anybody can remember and the only
signs of wealth or adequate income are those associated with the mer-
chants or trading post owners. They are the ones who settled in the
area, like the Mormons in Bluewater Valley, after the west was won.
After they had supplied and serviced the railroad contractors and mili-
tary, they arrived with wagonloads of merchandise and machinery and
set up business among the local poor.

Grants became a little city of 15,000 or so in the 1970's. After the
mid-'50s with the discovery of uranium in the Ambrosia Lake and
Laguna areas, it grew into a boom town. It was as drab and disorga-
nized and ill-planned as any boom town ever was. The Aacqumeh hanoh
nearby will attest to it; they are the ones whose irrigation and domes-
tic water was affected by the pollution caused by the sewage from the
city and its development. The clearest and most blatant example was
the Grants city sewage plant which sits right on the banks of the Rio
de San Jose which flows only twelve miles before it reaches the village
of Deetseyamah.

In the morning
I got up and prayed
and sang with what feeling
and meaning
I could remember:
    know this
    know that I mean well
    know that I am trying

344

    accept me, Earth, Sun,
    Spirit Powers of this land
    I am only a little person.
And then I climbed
to the flat top of Srhakaiya.
I surprised a buck deer.
Rather, we surprised each other.
Startled, it bounded away
and for a moment I ran after it,
laughing at how good it felt
to be there.
For the first time in twenty years,
it had rained early in the summer
and lightly sprinkled throughout.
And now there was such a profusion
of plants and flowers,
some I had never seen before.
    I ate a huuskahni,
the fruit of a yucca plant,
and some cactus fruit
which were not quite ripe.

The people at Aacqu talk about the days when grass was waist high.
It rained a lot then, elders say, and plants grew profusely and bore
fruits, seeds, food. Our people knew each plant, what its name was, its
particular features, and how it could be prepared for use. The people
knew many things.

It is certain and true that the people have known change for a long
time because there is always change. There was no time when there
was no change. There had to be. But people talk about how badly that
change came upon them and the land. In the oral tradition, war, crisis,
and famine are spoken about. The people had to cope with eras when
catastrophe came suddenly, inevitably, and perhaps necessarily when
the people had not paid careful heed to their responsibilities. They
speak about dissension among clans and within families. They note
the loss of good leadership, due to ineptitude and corruption and bad
judgment. The oral tradition does not ignore bad times and mistakes
that people have made throughout their history. And it is told in
mythic proportion in order to impress upon those hearing that there
are important lessons, values, and principles to be learned.

When corn, the cultivated seed and plant and food is spoken of, it is given a sacred nature because of the all-important item it is in the life of the people. It is a food, gift, seed, symbol, and it is the very essence of humankind's tending and nurturing of life, land, and product of physical, mental, and emotional work. Corn cannot be regarded as anything less than a sacred and holy and respected product of the creative forces of life, land, and the people's responsibilities and relationships. And when loss and waste are spoken of, it is in the same mythic proportion because it is totally serious business that life should not be destroyed. The Aacqumeh hanoh speak in the oral tradition about the certainty of life and growth and change. And just as certainly, they note there came a change that was bent upon a kind of destruction that was total and undeterred and over which they seemed to have no control.

I sat for a long time
on the high cliffs
on the western edge of Srhakaiya.
To the west lay the black lava beds.
That is the Gambler's fault.
That is the Monster's blood.
Aacqumeh hanoh and Dineh will tell you.
It must have been a tumultuous event.
I sat looking below
at the dirt road toward Quemado
and Pie Town, and Highway 117.
Several miles southward
was Qoweena springs
which formerly ran abundant.
Above the springs is a place
some ranchers named Robbers Roost.
It is an old Aacqumeh home.
    Ruins.
Robbers Roost—
what kind of name is that?
    The thieves.
    The thieves.

In August of 1680 when the Pueblo people rose against the ruling Spanish oppressor, they were joined in the revolt by the *mestizo* and *genizaro*, ancestors of the Chicano people, and the Athapascan-speaking peoples whose descendants are the peoples of the Navajo and Apache nations, and descendants of Africans who had been brought to the New World as slaves. They were all commonly impoverished. These people rebelled against the oppressive rule of the civil, church, and armed guard of the Spanish colonialist. They were forced to submit to the control of the wealthy and so-called royalty and religious fanatics who forbade native spiritual practice and beliefs because of the social integrity and strength upon which they were based. It took years of tolerance before it became crucial to organize resistance—a liberation struggle—against the oppressor. And when the revolt happened, it was successful in its intent, to drive away the destroyers and the thieves.

Later, in 1692, as De Vargas swept back brutally in bloody reconquest, he did not win total submission from the people. The Spaniard had to settle for tacit recognition of the people who would insist on their freedom. Although the Spaniard remained among the people until 1821 in the present-day Southwest, he was never the outright killer and thief that he was before the revolt.

As I started my climb
down from Srhakaiya,
I found a marker,
its head stamped
with an official seal and number.
Years ago, I was told
it is illegal to destroy
U.S. property.
My father told me.
    The markers are brass
set in concrete.

The Aacqumeh hanoh had never seen thieves like the Mericano before. They were so shrewd, talkative, even helpful, and so friendly they didn't look like thieves. As the Mericano stole unto the land, claiming it, the people didn't even feel like anything was being taken away from them. And they even blamed themselves and began to feel it was their fault. They couldn't or didn't speak English or write; that's why it turned out badly for them they decided.

347

Solomon Bibo, a merchant, married one of the women of Aacqu, and he opened his stores to the Pueblo. He and his brother became wealthy and powerful and the people grew indebted to them and dependent. The Aacqumeh hanoh suddenly found themselves with less land than before, especially on the northern boundary of their land near the merchant's store. They couldn't read documents written in English or speak fast and friendly enough, so Bibo spoke for them while he worked with U.S. surveyors who measured up the land in the 1880's. The thieves were sly, and the Aacqumeh hanoh like other Indians across the nation were in the hands of a ruthless, monopolistic U.S. empire.

Even in the darkest and most despairing era when disease, famine, loss of land and spirit burdened the Aacqumeh people from 1880 to the 1920's, they did not rise as they had two hundred years before. In fact this is true, most of the memory of that courageous liberation struggle had been erased from them, and they felt only a stasis that could not name an enemy though surely there was one.

The West had been won, and in the latter 19th century and into the 20th, the U.S. was settling in.

My father spoke
about the years
between 1914–1920.
    Dark years,
boyhood years.
    The people sick,
sunken with hunger,
loss, and grief.
    Terrified
of being totally alone,
orphaned.
His voice would drift
away.

The sun was so fierce
and its heat a weight
like a hot stone
on my shoulders
as I slowly made my way
    down.

Felt like Srhakaiya
was pushing me away.

I don't know when it was that the grass was as high as a man's
waist. I never knew that. All my life, the grass has been sparse and
brittle. All my life, the winters have been cold and windy and the
summers hot and mostly rainless. But the people talk about those good
days. I wonder. I think they mean those good years when they could
cope with life on their own terms. The winters were always cold and
the summers hot, but they could cope with them because there was a
system of life which spelled out exactly how to deal with the realities
they knew. The people had developed a system of knowledge which
made it possible for them to work at solutions. And they had the capa-
bilities of developing further knowledge to deal with new realities.
There was probably not anything they could not deal properly and
adequately with until the Mericano came.

The Mericano was stealthy in his approaches to the people. He
knew they could and would fight. He had found that out in the wars on
the Great Plains. Indian people could stop him cold and cost him mil-
lions of dollars and time. He could not bear to spend more money than
he had to nor time because he was so short-sighted. And so he became
a very smart thief.

Thomas Jefferson and Alexander Hamilton had spelled it out in po-
litical and economic theory: the U.S. needed capital for it to be really
considered a free and independent national power. Land was the only
real asset the U.S. had, and it would be the commodity used to raise
capital. And in the early 19th century, most of the present land was
in the possession of Indian people. So in the 1820's and the 1830's,
Andrew Jackson was sent to remove Indians from the land, and he was
made President because he was successful at it.

To cast away Indians was easy enough. Africans were already slaves
because they were strong and simple-minded, and Indians were uncivi-
lized and animalistic who needed civilizing. It was easy enough, and
there was even something called Manifest Destiny which ordained the
U.S. with a religious mission. There was no need for conspiracy to
steal and defraud; rather there was a national goal to fulfill and godly
purpose to be done. Laws, in fact, could be made and changed and new
ones made which would legally serve economic and social interests
with more proficiency.

The railroads were given grants of land by the U.S. which were Indian lands. Treaties were signed with Indian people who believed that the documents meant U.S. acceptance of their sovereign nations. To the railroads and the system of U.S. society which required capital, it was a simple matter of access and right of way and more land. The action swept on. Tecumseh, the Shawnee freedom fighter, was courageous in the early 19th century, and Osceola led his people desperately in the 1820's and 30's, both trying to save lands and people, and they were both killed. Crazy Horse organized a freedom movement on the Plains, and he was assassinated. Sitting Bull submitted and was paraded like a clown.

The nation swept on. The wash at Sand Creek in Colorado filled with Cheyenne and Arapahoe blood in 1864 and the reservation system and the Allotment Act were already in effect when the final hush settled as the Hotchkiss guns fell silent at Wounded Knee in 1891. The U.S. now claimed eminent domain and the proud steam locomotive train thundered across the vast American nation.

The Irishman, McCarty, would rise from his laboring class and be the man who pumped water from the chuna running through Aacqumeh land. A sign with his name would be erected beside the steel tracks by the railroad company.

The nation swept on into the 20th century and the Mericano was not called thief or killer; instead he was a missionary, merchant and businessman, philanthropist, educator, civil servant, and worker. Acoma: The Sky City would appear on state and national maps as a roadside attraction.

When I reached bottom
I was exhausted.
It was mid-afternoon.
Qoweena was too far away.
Stones were hot.
   I'd always been told
that water could be found.
I walked downstream
in the dry bed.
Hot stone.
Around the next bend,
there had to be water.
Under rock overhangs,

in depressions, under.
Stone.
　Blue blue dry sky.
Finally, I found water.

　The people insist on talking about the years when there was rain
and when the grass was lush and tall. It is not with mere nostalgia that
they speak, because it is not memory they refer to. Rather, it is a view
of the struggle that they have known. "The grass was tall and our ani-
mals had plenty to feed upon and we had great herds. But they poi-
soned the coyotes and prairie dogs. Then the barrenness began." In the
oral tradition, it is stated like that. "We had fields that produced more
than enough, chili, pumpkins, more than enough to share, but soon
there was less good land and less water. And it was because of them."
The oral tradition is very definite when it speaks upon the difficulties
that the people have undergone. "It is the rico," they say, "which has
taken from the people and the land."
　They are very sure who the rich are; they are the ones who have
money, possession, power, and the U.S. law on their side. The rico are
those who were associated with the railroad which took the land; they
are those who cause the people to become indebted and dependent; the
rico are the ones who turned the children away from the beliefs and
practices of the people. It is they who have used the Mericano power
and the law to control affairs that had been formerly the people's to
control.
　The people had always been able to deal with the earth, even its bar-
ren times, even its rainless times, on their own terms. But when the
Mericano system caused dependency, the people became bewildered
and often helpless and, at best, were only able to cope inadequately. In
the first several decades of the 20th century, the Aacqumeh hanoh
managed to continue farming and raising livestock, but more and more
they were pressured into leaving Aacqu for boarding school and to seek
work elsewhere. As the Santa Fe railroad laid its rails through Aac-
qumeh hahtse, as well as those of its sister, Kahwaika, to the east, it
gathered up men and employed them as unskilled labor and scattered
them along its route. Gallup, Winslow, Flagstaff, Needles, Barstow, Los
Angeles, Richmond became familiar names because that was where
Aacqumeh men worked. The productive labor devoted to farming and
livestock grew less, and the people became more dependent on a wage
income. In order to save family and clan life, many people went ahead

and relocated to colonies set up by the railroad company. In the 1940's and 1950's, there were many Aacqumeh families living in California.

This land yearns
for us.
The people yearn
for the land.
Loss and separation
are hard to bear.
   I walked those miles
on the dry stony floor
of the hot canyon
feeling I was being overcome
by some force
I did not know.
   Searing wind
into my mind.

In 1966, when the El Paso Natural Gas Company pipeline ruptured at Deechuna and shot exploding flames five hundred feet into the night sky, old man Shahrrowka said, "I had gotten up quite early, put wood in the stove, and I felt the light, but I knew it was not going to be sunrise yet. And then I looked, and the light was in the wrong place." And my father remembered an earlier time, "I got up that morning because the light was strange. It could not be the sun I thought to myself, and when I looked the light was too far to the south. It shimmered and faded, and it did not settle." I was only a few years old when the false dawn happened in 1945, rising out of the southeastern New Mexican plains. Some people recall the strange dawn as a tremor of light they could feel passing through them.

The railroads and the U.S. government which advocated for them had been pretty thorough. They wanted the land, and they took it. They wanted the people's labor, and they took it. It was not strange or out of character that they would awaken that New Mexico morning with an unsettling tremor of light that was the atomic blast at White Sands. One elder woman in discussing the gas line explosion in 1966 said, "I knew that they were up to something again. I knew they were going to do that. You come to expect it of them." The business of war came to Aacqumeh hanoh with the draft for World War II. A number of them died in the Death March on the Bataan peninsula, and many did not return as whole as they had left.

The people mourned the loss of their men because they had lost many of their children previously to mission and federal schools from where they were likely to return less than whole. The people would let them go, of course, after much counsel and advice, telling the young to rely upon the fundamental knowledge of their heritage. And they would grieve because there was always that chance of loss, but they let them go, telling them, "Hahtrudzaimeh, Qcumeh," for them to have courage and strength as men and women of their people. War was not new to the Aacqumeh hanoh, because they had known war before. They had been drawn into World War I by being told that if they served the U.S. their land and rights would be assured them. After the gasoline explosion in 1966, old man beloved Garcia spoke upon it, saying, "They told me if I served as a soldado for them, they would be grateful by protecting my land. But that was a lie—they are liars! Look at what they have done!"

Although the people have known the experience and difficulty of loss, they did not understand the meaning of that strange dawn in 1945 and in some ways they still don't. And it is because U.S. society doesn't understand either and refuses to deal with it. Thorough knowledge was what was always required to live by for Indian people, but since the Mericano, knowledge has been kept in some hidden place and has been used as controlling power. Although the people had felt the tremor of light and knew that it was strange, they did not know what it meant. The great majority of U.S. society did not know what it meant either, because knowledge was kept away from them just as effectively, and in many ways more so. The meaning was known only by a few people in the U.S. government, and to those who were in control of this knowledge, it meant power. They not only had power by controlling knowledge, but they had it by having the power to destroy.

In the Grants area for years it was popular knowledge that Paddy Martinez, a Navajo Indian, had discovered uranium. They said he brought a green stone to the attention of someone in Grants and it contained uranium ore. But that's not quite true. Grants and the U.S. system would have us believe it was as simple as that: it would reiterate the idea of the Indian bringing his own fate upon his head. There were any number of explorations for uranium since the 1940's in New Mexico. Oil, gas, and coal had been found and developed on the Navajo homeland since the 1920's, and it was common knowledge that they were profitable to exploit because of their location and the ready supply of labor. There was knowledge there were substantial uranium ore bodies in the Southwest, and all they needed was time to make a "discovery" and a place where there would be no problem in exploiting.

It was no exceptional decision that Los Alamos Laboratories were located where they were nor where the atomic bomb would be exploded. This was the remote barren west afterall, and only a few Indians were there. Therefore, uranium was "discovered" in the Four Corners region of the Southwest on and near Indian lands. There was no conspiracy involved either because it was unnecessary. This was the momentum of capitalism and its need to be continually profitable or else collapse. It had been going on since the era of Jacksonian democracy and the Seventh Cavalry and the setup of the reservation and land allotment system. The railroads had found it was easy enough to take land and water and labor because of the ties between business and the U.S. government. And now the Atomic Energy Commission would deal with the Department of Interior which had the Bureau of Indian Affairs and Bureau of Mines within it. It would be in the national interest, of course, with the U.S. economy at stake that Indian lands and people, whose affairs were ruled by the BIA, would be exploited. It was the west afterall, barren and undeveloped, with only a few vanishing red men and jackrabbits on it.

No, it was not that Navajo man who discovered uranium. It was the U.S. government and economic and military interests which would make enormous profits and hold the world at frightened bay which made that discovery in a colonized territory.

I met Emmett
herding sheep.
   He still walked
with a tense crouch.
Had a .22 rifle
slung across his back.
"Dark last night," he said,
"I shot at something,
Maybe a coyote;
maybe something."

He was far away
from Vietnam now.
But he was still close,
    close.
"You take care," I said.

In the early 1950's, Anaconda opened the ground north of Kahwaika.
All the time since it was formed, the land on the east slopes of Tsebi-
nah, as the Kahwaikameh hanoh call Kaweshtima, was mesa, canyon,
and grassland. Paguate village people had gardens and fields at the
mouths of canyons and arroyos and alongside the small stream from
the mountain. It had been like that for ages, but now the machines and
Mericanos in hardhats came.

Mining agreements were made between the Kawaikameh leadership
and the BIA, which was within the hold of the Department of Interior.
And the international mining company worked efficiently and quickly
after that. The Anaconda engineers surveyed and plotted, and soon
they drilled the stone, filled the drill holes with dynamite, and blasted.
And pushed the rubble away. They did it over and over again, until the
land was just so much rubble pushed aside to find the strata of ura-
nium bearing ore. It looked just like any gray and brown dirt and slabs
of rock, but it had a value that was based on power. And that power
could destroy in a way that not only had to do with savage and brute
force but with the way it would face Indian people upon whose land
mining and milling would take place with the question of survival.

There are songs
about the rain,
so beautiful.
White soft mist,
gentle on the land,
flowing in rivulets,
stone, shining,
so beautiful.
There are songs.

Kerr-McGee even earlier than Anaconda's development on Laguna
land had already begun mining and milling in the Cove and Shiprock
area in northwest New Mexico. It had the same pattern. Navajo people

had a small farming economy but most of their livelihood was in rais-
ing sheep; i.e., for those people who did have some. It was bare subsis-
tence, and most Navajo people were faced with unemployment and
dependency on welfare which was begrudgingly meted out and used
to control the people. The Navajo men who went into the under-
ground mines did not have much choice except to work there, just like
the Laguna miners who found themselves as surface labor and semi-
skilled workers. The Kerr-McGee underground mines were dusty, and
in twenty years the Navajo miners who had stayed for any length of
time underground breathing the dust laden with radon gas would find
themselves cancerous. The Laguna miners would find themselves
questioning how much real value the mining operation had when their
land was overturned into a gray pit miles and miles in breadth. They
would ask if the wages they earned, causing wage income dependency,
and the royalties received by the Kawaikah people were worth it when
Mericano values beset their children and would threaten the heritage
they had struggled to keep for so long.

Walking away
from Srhakaiya
I remembered 1952.
The Felipe brothers
had risen and tried
to stem state power.
Desperate.
Action.
    Hot and thirsty
again, clouds
in the northwest
toward Ambrosia Lake
no hope at all.
They killed the state
cop, southeast
of Srhakaiya.

Right out of high school I worked in the mining and milling region
of Ambrosia lake. I was nineteen years old. My father, like others, had
worked for the railroad for years, as a laborer on section crews and a
welder on extra gangs. Most of the railroad workers I ever saw were
Indians, Indo-Hispanos, and Blacks, with occasional Okies, and the

foremen were always white. My father firmly said that he did not wish for me and my brothers to ever work for the Santa Fe railroad. We were to go to school, get an education, and find something that was not grueling labor. He was like other Indian fathers who spoke about education which would help the people. He did not himself have much, and so he believed in education. That would be the answer, and it would be a weapon with which we would fight. But we were poor, and education beyond high school was not a likely opportunity though the BIA offered relocation to on-the-job training and work in the cities.

Some Aacqumeh high school graduates went on BIA relocation or entered military service, which is another refuge for the poor, but I decided to work. We had always been poor, though sometimes it didn't feel like it except we knew we didn't have much and were always envious of others who had more. One of the things we said, it seemed like constantly, and we heard even our elders saying it, was "Gaimuu Mericano," speaking of the good fortune of being a white American. We were resentful too, of course, though at nineteen I didn't know intellectually why or how that was the case, except that at times angrily we would seek out Indo-Hispanos and whites to fight. We knew we were close to the bottom of the social scale, and we knew that was a scary and painful place to be. So I went to work at Ambrosia Lake.

Mostly, I worked at the Kerr-McGee millsite although several times I went underground into the mines. At the mill, I worked in crushing, leaching, and yellowcake, usually at various labor positions but later as an operator which was not much different or more skilled than laborer. I had a job, and for poor people with low education and no skills and high unemployment, that is the important thing: a job. In 1960, some subsistence farming on small garden plots was still done at Aacqu, but faced with the U.S. economy and its impact, a wage income was becoming necessary. Like the railroad, mining had an impact though not immediately because Indian men were not readily hired at the mines and mills. But after the wildcat strike at Ambrosia Lake in 1961 more Indians were hired because we were the surplus labor, and the exploited Okies, West Virginians, and oilfield workers from the Gulf were trying to get organized. The strike actually saved me from spending a lifetime at the mines, because I went to college before the strike ended. But many Aacqumeh men continued to work at Ambrosia Lake as underground and surface miners with a few at the millsites.

Mining is dangerous work, whether underground or surface, but people continued to work there because there was no other employment available. It was total and intensive work, and the New Mexican and national economy required it. It was not the safety or health or lives of the miners there was concern for. In the national interest, mine operators, oil corporations, utility companies, international energy cartels, and investors sacrificed these men and women. In the Grants Uranium Belt area, which is the area between Albuquerque and Gallup, there was a miner killed every month. At home in Aacqu, there are former miners who walk around crippled, as maimed as if they had been wounded in wartime.

At moments, during the struggle in the 1970's and 1980's in the Southwest, I got paranoid about my own health. In 1960, there was no information about the dangers of radiation from yellowcake with which I worked. I didn't know if workers got any more information or warnings than we did twenty years before. The company managers and superintendents knew something or at least scientists did, but they didn't allow for its dissemination. If they did pass it on, it was low key, and it must have been low key in 1980 because there didn't seem to be much worker organizing for safer handling of yellowcake. But twenty years later, I worried about it, and I got angry because there weren't any special precautions we were required or urged to take then.

In the milling operation at the end of the leaching and settling process, the yellow liquid was drawn into dryers which took the water out. The dryers were screen constructions which revolved slowly in hot air; yellow pellets were extruded and crushed into a fine powder. The workers were to keep the machinery operating, which was never smooth, and most of the work involved was to keep it in free operation; i.e., frequently having to unclog it by hand. There was always a haze of yellow dust flying around, and even though filtered masks were used, the workers breathed in the fine dust. It got in their hair and cuts and scratches and in their eyes. I was nineteen then, and twenty years later I worried about it.

On the way to Srahkaiya
the day before,
I had met old man
beloved Bowtuwah
above his sheep camp.
He told me about some hawks
nesting in the cliffs nearby.

358

When I was a boy,
Bowtuwah would bring his sheep
to water at the chuna,
the Rio de San Jose,
and we would run
to greet him every time
he did so.
Uncle, we would call,
how are you?
Fine, he would say,
and he would laugh.
He was a kind, gentle,
and funny man, younger then.
And he would always
tell us stories and jokes.

Once he told us,
it was true he said,
that in the olden times,
the people ate dragonflies.
Dragonflies, we cried.
Yes, he said, fine food,
tasty, fixed a certain way.
No, we said, Arreh-eh.
Yes, he said, in the olden times.
We wanted to hear
about the olden times,
and he would tell us.
It's true, Bowtuwah
would say, it's all true.
    Later, he would have us
chasing dragonflies
up and down the river,
trying to catch
at least one,
but they were always too fast.
If you can catch
the fastest one,
that will be the tastiest
he would say, laughing.

Well, I better go see
if my sheep haven't
all drowned.

He is gone now,
and sometimes I wish
he were still with us
and I was a boy
listening
to stories
by the river,
all of us laughing.

The struggle goes on and it will continue. It is in the stories of the
oral tradition and the advice and counsel that it will go on.

The Southwestern U.S. is caught in the throes of economic ventures
and political manipulation which are ultimately destructive if the U.S.
government and the multi-national corporations do not have people
and the land and their continuance as their foremost concern. It is not
a matter of higher income for Indians because there will be higher in-
comes as inflation goes higher. It is not a matter of a higher standard of
living which we are led to seek as the only possible alternative. It is
survival that is at stake and it is the quality of life that is at stake. It is
the survival of not only the Aacqumeh hanoh or the Dineh or other
Southwestern native peoples, but it is all people of this nation. If the
survival and quality of the life of Indian peoples is not assured, then no
one else's life is, because those same economic, social, and political
forces which destroy them will surely destroy others. It is not only a
matter of preserving and protecting Indian lands as some kind of natu-
ral wilderness or cultural parks; rather it is a matter of how those
lands can be productive in terms which are Indian people's to make,
instead of Indian people being forced to serve a U.S. national interest
which has never adequately served them. Those lands can be produc-
tive to serve humanity, just like the oral tradition of the Aacqumeh
hanoh says, and the people can be productive and serve the land so that
it is not wasted and destroyed.

But it will take real decisions and actions and concrete understand-
ing by the poor and workers of this nation. They will have to see that
the present exploitation of coal at Black Mesa Mine in Arizona does
not serve the Hopi and the Navajo whose homeland it is. They will

have to understand that the political and economic forces which have caused Hopi and Navajo people to be in conflict with each other and within their own nations are the same forces which steal the human fabric of their own American communities and lives. They will have to be willing to identify capitalism for what it is, that it is destructive and uncompassionate and deceptive.

They will have to be willing to do so or they will never understand why the Four Corners power plants in northwestern New Mexico continue to spew poisons into the air, destroying plant, animal, and human life in the area. They will have to be willing to face and challenge the corporations at their armed bank buildings, their stock brokers, and their drilling, mining, milling, refining and processing operations. If they don't do that, they will not understand what Aacqu and her sister Pueblos in the Southwest are fighting for when they seek time and time again to bring attention to their struggle for land, water, and human rights.

The American poor and the workers and white middleclass, who are probably the most ignorant of all U.S. citizens, must understand how they, like Indian people, are forced to serve a national interest, controlled by capitalist vested interests in collusion with U.S. policy makers, which does not serve them. Only when this understanding is attained and decisions are reached and actions taken to overcome economic and political oppression imposed upon all of us will there be no longer a national sacrifice area in the Southwest. Only then will there be no more unnecessary sacrifices of our people and land.

That feeling
of "otherness"
came on as I lay
in the shade
of a juniper.
It passed,
and I got up
and walked
into a canyon
which would
enter into a valley.
As I walked
into the valley
I saw some horses.

One was a pinto
and the other was red.
The sun had long set.
The horses were alert
to me as I passed by.
Suddenly, they bolted,
and galloped
into the canyon
toward Srahkaiya.
I watched them
until they vanished
into the folds
of the evening earth
that was the canyon
entering into
the dark near mountain
Srahkaiya.

In 1980, there were 43 uranium mines operating in the Grants
Uranium Belt and 5 mills. According to a BIA study, 107 mines and
21 mills would be in operation by the year 2000 in the Belt and the
San Juan Basin. Uranium yellowcake production in New Mexico was
9.7 million pounds in 1977; it was to have increased to 24.1 million
in 1980. There were 31 companies exploring for and developing ura-
nium in New Mexico. Kerr-McGee, Conoco, Gulf, Mobil, Phillips,
TVA, Pioneer Nuclear and United Nuclear are all energy corporations;
they were all there. Mobil and TVA were planning *in situ* mining in
which chemicals are pumped into drill holes, interacting with ura-
nium ore bodies deep in the earth, and the solution is pumped out and
processed.

The 43 mines in the late 1970's were dewatering, because most of
the underground ore bodies were wet, between 190,000 to 250,000
gallons per minute. Nevertheless, even with all this activity, it was un-
certain that peak production would continue as even then mines were
closing and workers being laid off, causing even more economic dis-
tress for the people in the area. In fact, by the early 1980's uranium ore
extracting and processing was drastically reduced, and there was al-
most none going on by the 1990's. The market for uranium had dropped,
some of it due to concerns and protests about radiation hazards and
pollution.

This much is certain now however: the people of Deetseyamah and Deechuna and Kahwaikah downstream from the Grants Uranium Belt do not have enough water any more for their few remaining cultivated fields and gardens, and the water they drink is contaminated by Grants and the past processing mills. The hanoh anxiously watch the springs at Ghoomi and Gaanipah. Their struggle will go on; there is no question about that.

We must have passionate concern for what is at stake. We must understand the experience of the oppressed, especially the racial and ethnic minorities, of this nation, by this nation and its economic interests. Only when we truly understand and accept the responsibilities of that understanding will we be able to make the necessary decisions for change. Only then will we truly understand what it is to love the land and people and to have compassion. Only when we are not afraid to fight against the destroyers, thieves, liars, exploiters who profit handsomely off the land and people will we know what love and compassion are. Only when the people of this nation, not just Indian people, fight for what is just and good for all life, will we know life and its continuance. And when we fight, and fight back those who are bent on destruction of land and people, we will win. We will win.

A New Story

Several years ago,
I was a patient at the VA hospital
in Ft. Lyons, Colorado.
I got a message to call this woman,
so I called her up.
She said to me,
"I'm looking for an Indian.
Are you an Indian?"
"Yes," I said.

"Oh good," she said,
"I'll explain why I'm looking
for an Indian."
And she explained.
"Every year, we put on a parade
in town, a Frontier Day Parade.
It's exciting and important,
and we have a lot of participation."
"Yes," I said.
"Well," she said, "Our theme
is Frontier,
and we try to do it well.
In the past, we used to make up
paper mache Indians,
but that was years ago."
"Yes," I said.
"And then more recently,
we had some people
who dressed up as Indians
to make it more authentic,
you understand, real people."
"Yes," I said.
"Well," she said,
"that didn't seem right,
but we had a problem.
There was a lack of Indians."
"Yes," I said.
"This year, we wanted to do it right.
We have looked hard and high
for Indians but there didn't seem
to be any in this part of Colorado."
"Yes," I said.
"We want to make it real, you understand,
put a real Indian on a float,
not just a paper mache dummy
or an Anglo dressed as an Indian
but a real Indian with feathers and paint.
Maybe even a medicine man."
"Yes," I said.

"And then we learned the VA hospital
had an Indian here.
We were so happy,"
she said, happily.
"Yes," I said.
"there are several of us here."
"Oh good," she said.

Well, last Spring
I got another message
at the college where I worked.
I called the woman.
She was so happy
that I returned her call.
And then she explained
that Sir Francis Drake,
the English pirate
(she didn't say that, I did)
was going to land on the coast
of California in June, again.
And then she said
she was looking for Indians . . .
"No," I said. No.

ABOUT THE AUTHOR

SIMON J. ORTIZ, poet, short fiction writer, essayist, and lately a documentary and feature filmwriter, is a native of Acoma Pueblo. He lives at Deetseyamah, a rural community west of Albuquerque, New Mexico. As a major, influential Native American writer, he eloquently expresses the living story of his people, a story often marred by social, political, and economic conflicts with Anglo American society. Yet, like Native American oral tradition, which always stresses the possibility of vision and hope through creative struggle and resistance, Ortiz's poetry and fiction engage readers and listeners and invite their involvement and commitment. *Woven Stone* includes three previously published books of poetry and prose and an extensive introductory essay about their evolvement.